THE NEW ENGLAND QUILT MUSEUM

QUILTS

*Featuring the Story
of the Mill Girls*

Instructions for
Five Heirloom
Quilts

JENNIFER GILBERT

C&T PUBLISHING

Developmental Editor: *Cyndy Lyle Rymer*
Technical Editor: *Sara Kate MacFarland*
Copy Editing: *Vera Tobin* and
    Barbara Konzak Kuhn
Book Design: *Irene Morris*
Cover Production: *Christina Jarumay*
Cover Design: *Christina Jarumay*
Graphic Illustrations: *Jay Richards*
Cover Photo by *David Caras*
Back Cover Photo by *Greg Heins*
Photography by *Ken Burris* except where
otherwise noted.

**Library of Congress
Cataloging-in-Publication Data**

Gilbert, Jennifer.
The New England Quilt Museum quilts :
featuring the story of the mill girls :
instructions for five heirloom quilts /
Jennifer Gilbert.
    p. cm.
    Includes bibliographical references
    (p.) and index.
    ISBN 1-57120-075-4 (paper trade)
    1. Quilts—United States—Catalogs.
    2. New England Quilt Museum—
    Catalogs. I. Title.
NK9112 .G52 1999
746.46'0973'0747444—ddc21   99-6127
                        CIP

Published by C&T Publishing, Inc.,
P.O. Box 1456, Lafayette, California 94549

Printed in Hong Kong
10 9 8 7 6 5 4 3 2 1

Acknowledgments

No publication is possible without the support of many friends. The New England Quilt Museum was founded and is still supported by the fellowship of quilters. I would first like to thank the staff and many volunteers who give a tremendous amount of themselves to support the institution. Thanks goes to Adeline Alkan, Eric and Isobel Baade, Ben and Mary Curtis, Marcia Learmonth, Joan Terry, and Alice Wiggin for helping me design and install the exhibitions; Charlotte Feldman, Ann Penn and Martha Supnik of the Marjorie Dannis Library at the NEQM; Rhoda Cohen, Nancy Halpern, and many other artists for lending me their expert advice and insights about the modern quilt. Many thanks to those individuals and guilds who have donated quilt treasures to the museum, especially Gail Binney-Stiles and the Binney family, whose gifts made the museum the quality institution it is today. Many thanks to former board member Stephanie Hatch for her in-depth curatorial observations that added insight into my understanding of the quilts in the permanent collection. Finally, I want to thank my family and friends for supporting my fascination with quilts.

Jennifer Gilbert

Attention Teachers: *C&T Publishing, Inc. encourages you to use this book as a text for teaching. Contact us at 800-284-1114 or www.ctpub.com for more information about the C&T Teachers Program.*

CONTENTS

DETAIL FROM NORTH BY NORTHEAST.
Designed by Paula Libby.

Historical Background

Gallery

Projects

Foreword

by Patricia Steuert, Executive Director, New England Quilt Museum

NORTH BY NORTHEAST, 1994.
97 ¼" x 98", designed by Paula Libby.
Cotton, machine pieced, hand appliquéd,
and hand quilted by members of the
Evergreen Chapter of the Pine Tree
Quilters Guild of Maine.
Gift of the Pine Tree Quilters Guild, 1995.18.

The story of quilting is rooted in the lives of American women: from the earliest settlers in New England, to the nineteenth century "mill girls" who produced the cloth, to the fifteen million quilters today. The focus of this book is the imagination, perseverance, and community spirit that infuses the history of quilting. The story comes alive in our accounts of the "mill girls," the New England Quilt Museum, and its hometown of Lowell, Massachusetts.

What is it about quilting that makes it so much a part of the story of America? Mention the word quilt to almost anyone and you will hear stories of their grandmother who made quilts in the past, or friends today who are contemporary quilters. You will also hear about family heirlooms packed for a journey to a new home, bringing with them the history and memories of a past culture. The richness of the quilting experience reflects the scope of this art and craft—an art form that crosses cultural backgrounds and social classes.

While the function of quilts has changed, quilting is still an integration of women's desire for creative self-expression, intellectual and artistic challenge, social companionship, and community involvement.

Whether alone or in guilds, quilters today create traditional and contemporary quilts for themselves, their businesses, or for others using a range of simple supplies to programmable computers. The New England Quilt Museum is proud to collect and preserve this important history. We are creating a place and community for the next generation of quilters.

DETAIL OF MARINER'S COMPASS,
1880–1900.
Anonymous, probably Massachusetts,
77 ½" x 73 ¾", cotton, hand pieced
and quilted.
Gift of The Binney Family, 1987.03.

New England Quilt Museum History

by Patricia Steuert

In the years surrounding the United States Bicentennial of 1976, quilting experienced an enormous renaissance. With the help of guilds to create hundreds of commemorative quilts, museums offered exhibitions to celebrate the occasion.

A few years later, a group of women in New England shared a vision of quilting that extended beyond the historical celebration, one with a promising and exciting future. These were the early members of the New England Quilters Guild (NEQG) who worked together to raise awareness of quilting by organizing quilt shows and workshops.

Janet Elwin, a quilter and teacher from Maine and one-time president of NEQG, inspired this group to dream of the day when there would be a showplace for their craft, a permanent place to preserve and interpret the history of quiltmaking in New England.

Between 1981 and 1986 these early NEQG leaders promoted their ideas for a museum and raised funds for their dream. They founded the New England Quilt Museum in 1987 to preserve the region's quilt heritage. Their goal was to establish an institution devoted solely to quilts, a place where quilts would be preserved, studied, and celebrated. In making plans to serve quilters and the general public, the founders placed primary emphasis on exhibition and education. The intent was to provide a complete story of quiltmaking, from traditional domestic craft to contemporary fine art.

Their dream took root in a recycled brick mill building on Market Street, in Lowell. Museum staff and many volunteers spent the following four years showcasing the all-encompassing character of quilting with six to eight annual exhibitions.

Then in 1991 a flood forced the museum out of the Market Mills building. Temporary shelter was found in the clock tower of the Boott Cotton Mills where the museum remained until 1993 when the Board of Directors of the NEQM purchased the Lowell Institution for Savings Bank building on Shattuck Street. This building has significance in that it was the first bank that encouraged "mill girls", those women who worked in the mills, to save their wages.

NEQM NOW.
Photo by James Higgins.

Background Photo:
BANK BUILDING, C. 1851.
Courtesy of University of Massachusetts, Lowell.

Master craftsman Josiah Peabody built the Lowell Institute for Savings building in 1845 in the classic Greek Revival style. The structure boasts an unusual rhomboidal footprint, with curved corners and an ornate wrought-iron balcony along two sides. Today the 18,000 square foot space holds exhibition galleries, a library and resource center, classrooms, a museum store, collection storage, staff offices, and support areas. Because of its previous function as a bank it also contains three large vaults that are always of interest to visiting tourists.

Left: BACK FROM THE FLOOD BROCHURE, curated by Jennifer Gilbert for the opening exhibition at 18 Shattuck Street.

Lowell is a prime location for a quilt museum. Many of the fabrics used in nineteenth century American quilts were woven in the city's mills. The city is also an important site for women's history because most of the early mill workers were women. The Lowell National Historical Park maintains sites throughout the city and houses the Boott Cotton Mills Museum, which chronicles the social history of life in the mills. The American Textile History Museum, which relocated to Lowell in April of 1997, tells a complete history of textile manufacturing in America. This combination of local resources improves the value of all three institutions for historians, researchers, quilters, and the general public. The New England Quilt Museum, one of several museums in the nation dedicated solely to quilts, has taken its place as part of the cultural industry of Lowell.

THE MUSEUM COLLECTION

"BUY A BRICK" MURAL.

In 1997, to celebrate its tenth anniversary a quilt mural was painted on the backside of the NEQM building. Enjoyed by all visitors to the city, the mural is a symbol for those who contributed to the "Buy a Brick" capital campaign. This campaign began in 1995 to pay down the mortgage on the building since the carrying costs were putting a strain on the small operating budget. This was truly a broad-based campaign with participation from individual guilds from all six New England states, and fabric-related businesses across the United States, as well as Germany and Japan. With a leadership gift from Joan Fabrics of Lowell and a grant from the Theodore Edson Parker Foundation, the mortgage was retired in May 1998.
Photo by Robert Bullerwell.

The New England Quilt Museum began with a small collection of primarily donated quilts. This early collection included several antique quilts as well as two contemporary pieces commissioned by the New England Quilters Guild. In 1991, the Binney family donated 33 antique quilts, forming the core of the museum's permanent collection. This gift, which included representative samples from all eras of quilt history, added breadth and depth to the NEQM collection.

Gail Binney-Stiles, a painter and graphic artist, and her father, Edwin Binney III, a Harvard professor and avid art collector, shared a fondness for quilts with bold color contrasts, as shown in their impressive selection of Amish and Mennonite quilts. Edwin's preference for graphic design was satisfied with a number of indigo and white quilts, while Gail appreciated the magnificent piecing, appliqué, and fine hand quilting represented in two-color quilts. Not only did Gail donate these quilts to the museum, but she also provided resources to leverage additional support for the museum's collection. Gail Binney-Stiles' generosity continues as every year she donates a quilt from her collection to the museum, which boasts over 42 quilts from the Binney family collection.

The museum has been given significant New England quilts by generous individuals and families seeking to preserve their textile histories. The museum's collection has also grown due to the generosity of New England quilt guilds, who have given contemporary and traditional quilts to our permanent collection. They have also donated quilts to use as fundraisers for the purchase and care of our antique quilts. The entire museum collection today includes over 150 quilts and quilt tops, ranging from "All White" made in 1808 to "Bee Balm Screen" (1982) by Ruth McDowell, a highly regarded contemporary New England quilter.

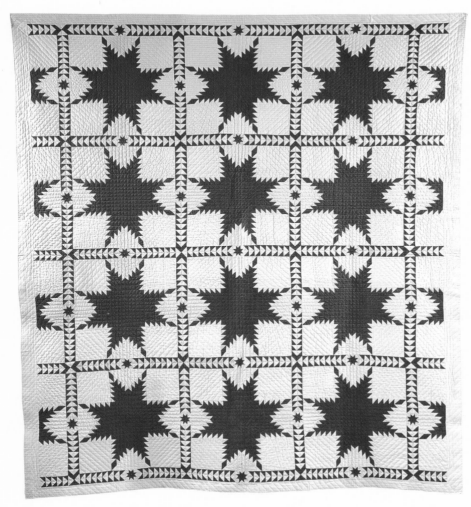

FEATHERED STAR WITH WILD GOOSE CHASE
AND EIGHT-POINTED STAR SASHING,
1850–1870.
Origin unknown, 73 ½" x 80 ½",
cotton, hand pieced and quilted.
Gift of The Binney Family, 1991.05.

This quilt first appeared on the cover of
Carleton Safford and Robert Bishop's book of
quilt history, *America's Quilts and Coverlets.*
The quilt was later bought by the Binneys,
who donated it to the NEQM.

Since the New England Quilt Museum opened in 1987, over 150,000
people have been inspired by more than sixty different exhibitions,
displaying quilts in a broad range of eras, styles, and techniques.
To complement these exhibitions, a variety of educational programs
are held for school classes, guilds, and beginning to advanced quilters.
Lectures from guest artists with accompanying slide shows, workshops,
and gallery tours give extra meaning to the exhibitions. Sally Palmer
Field, an expert on New England quilts and mill fabrics, has taught
many people the basics of quilting using examples from her personal
collection. School classes visiting the museum often request a "hands
on" workshop to provide background for their gallery tour. Members
of the NEQM staff also teach "The Geometry of Quilting" as part of a
summer institute for public school teachers in Massachusetts. Along with
other cultural institutions in Lowell, the museum provides workshops
for families and children during school vacations and holidays.

BEE BALM SCREEN, 1982.
Ruth McDowell, Winchester,
Massachusetts, 117" x 67", cotton, blends,
metallics. Machine pieced and hand quilted.
Gift of The Binney Family, 1997.04.

MINI-BASKET, C. 1895.
Anonymous, New England, 84 ½" x 91",
cotton, hand appliquéd and quilted.
Gift of The Binney Family, 1991.34.

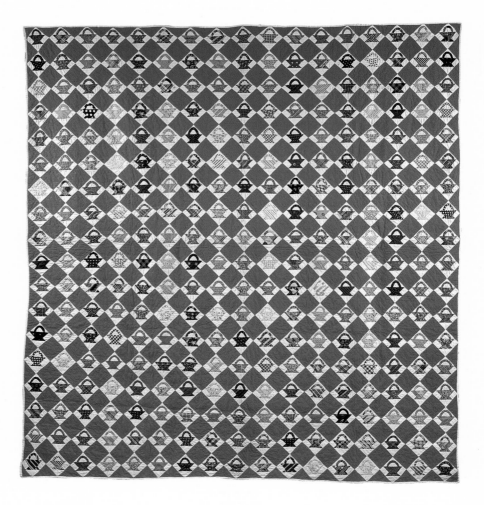

The museum shop boasts one of the most comprehensive collections of quilt-related books and gift items and provides operating income for the museum. The museum library, founded by a large donation of resources from Marjorie Dannis, a professional librarian, is volunteer-staffed and self-funding. Library staff also maintain the museum's website at http://www.NEQuiltMuseum.org.

The museum is a resource for everyone interested in quilts: including quilters, collectors, researchers, and teachers. Tourists from every state in the United States, and visitors from England to South Africa to Japan, view American treasures rarely on display in other museums. The NEQM continues its mission into the new century with the support of all the people who share its vision. An endowment to support the museum and its collection is in the planning phase. These funds will assure that whatever economic forces prevail on the "textile city," the dream of the early founders of the New England Quilt Museum will survive.

ALBUM SUMMER COVERLET, C. 1850.
Anonymous, probably New York, 101" x 87",
cotton, hand appliquéd and embroidered.
Gift of The Binney Family, 1991.15.

LOWELL AND THE MILL GIRLS

As European settlers arrived in Massachusetts and moved inland, they traded with the Indians of the Pennacook Confederacy who controlled most of the territory that is now Lowell. The settlers forced the relocation of many of the Indians in their desire for the fertile land on theMerrimack and Concord Rivers.

In 1685, settlers acquired the land that had been set aside for the Indians and established Chelmsford. Lowell remained part of Chelmsford until it became an independent city in 1826.

Industrialization swept through America in the early nineteenth century, transforming its people and their customs. Industry dramatically changed the lives of the New England women who entered the workforce in Lowell, Massachusetts, and of the immigrant women and men who followed in their footsteps. The history of Lowell is the story of the beginning of the textile industry in America.

LOWELL IN 1825 by Benjamin Mather (1776-1863). Oil painting on stretched canvas, 32" x 47".

Gift of Philip S. Marden. Courtesy of the Whistler House Museum of Art, Lowell, Massachusetts.

CITY OF LOWELL'S OFFICIAL SEAL.

Courtesy of Lowell National Historical Park.

For more than a century before the first large cotton factories were built, the people of rural New England lived in a slow-paced, agrarian society. Their lives were attuned to the seasons, and households were self-sufficient. Women in colonial America carried out much of the domestic manufacturing, especially tasks centered around textile production. Until the nineteenth century those tasks were confined within a household setting. Women enjoyed a respected place in the family economy and were seen as managers of the home. Work was demanding, and both men and women worked six days a week, with only Sunday off for the Sabbath. New England winters are long, and the early primitive heating systems necessitated warm clothing and bedding. The family farm produced raw materials such as wool and flax, which women carded, spun, and wove. Not only farmers' wives, but women of all classes, created clothing and textiles for the home.

Background Photo:

YOUNG MILL WORKERS, C. 1860.

Courtesy of the American Textile History Museum.

Diaries of upper-class women from New England indicate that considerable time was spent sewing. Girls were taught to sew at a young age, and unmarried daughters were often sent to the homes of neighbors to assist with the quilting of petticoats and bedcovers.[1] The elaborate quilts that survive were made primarily by the wealthy, as fabric was expensive and time was dear.

Farmers' daughters would go out to work for wages as servants or seamstresses. Farm women frequently sold their work on a piecework basis, and the sale of goods to small factories and merchants for store credit was an important part of farm economy. Most of the product was textile-related, such as cotton yarn and braided split palm leaf, which was used for men's and children's hats.

INDUSTRIALIZATION

Until the early nineteenth century, textiles were either imported from Europe or woven in small mills in America. Under colonial law it was illegal to transport plans for the textile machinery used in England. In the early 1800s, Frances Cabot Lowell went to England to study British mill machinery; he memorized the designs and returned to his Boston studio to re-create the power loom. Lowell established the first fully integrated textile mill in Waltham, Massachusetts in 1813, and after technology proved itself in Waltham, factories began to spring up all over New England. By 1840 there were 700 cotton mills in villages and towns scattered throughout New England and along the rivers in the Northeast; and between 1790 and 1860 these mills were the largest employers of women.[2]

Lowell was a spotlight of early American invention and entreupreneurship. The ingenious system of locks and canals provided power to individually owned mills along the Merrimac River. The five-mile network of power canals solved the problem of how to harness natural power. This power drove the machines of the industrial age and helped give birth to the Industrial Revolution. The factories combined people with resources, and ideas with a market for cotton goods. Lowell became internationally known as a model for factory life and for the "mill girl" experiment.

The factories of Lowell were not only a revolution in technology, but one in labor history. By the 1830s the primary economic activity of the farmers' daughters—spinning and weaving—was made obsolete by the growing textile industry. The workers initially solicited by the mills were the young unmarried daughters of Yankee farmers, who came mostly from Maine, New Hampshire, and Vermont. Many women from rural communities moved to towns like Lowell for specific monetary goals, and spent an average of one to three years in the mills to make money to send home, to buy nice clothes, or save for a dowry. It was said that a quarter of all the young men who attended Harvard University were sent there with the help of money earned by their hard-working sisters in Lowell.[3]

A SMALL PART OF LOWELL'S "MILE OF MILLS" POISED OVER THE MERRIMAC RIVER.
Photo by James Higgins

The self-sufficient farm was dying out, and young women flocked to the region for the opportunity to earn a good living and become part of the young and thriving nation. The new scale of operations involved workers moving to factory towns; the Cooperatives made the cities appealing to these young women who were about to enjoy their first taste of economic and social independence.

THE BOARDINGHOUSE COMMUNITY

To house the mill girls, the companies built scores of boardinghouses. In the mid-1830s nearly three-fourths of the female workers lived in boardinghouses, usually under the charge of responsible older women.

Yet another feature that distinguished the Lowell mills in this period was the monthly payment of cash wages. Most other employers paid workers with credit at a company store or settled wages four times a year. In Lowell during the 1830s, a woman might earn $12 to $14 a month. After paying $5 monthly for room and board in a company boardinghouse, she had the rest for clothing, tickets to lectures, savings, or incidentals. She could never have earned this much money at farm work and quite likely had more ready cash than her father. It was common for young women to return home after a year in the mills with $25 to $50 in a bank account.

RESIDENTS OF A BOOTT MILLS
BOARDINGHOUSE, C. 1880.

A group stands in front of what is thought to be a Boott Mills boardinghouse in the 1870s.
Courtesy of Lowell National Historical Park.

SPINNING ROOM AT
BOOTT COTTON MILLS, C. 1910.
Courtesy of Lowell National Historical Park.

UNIDENTIFIED PORTUGUESE MILL WORKER,
C. 1910.

Courtesy of University of Massachusetts, Lowell.

Wages were not Lowell's sole attraction for women. The city also offered social, cultural, and religious opportunities. In evenings after work, the women might attend a lecture, exhibition, or play. They could subscribe to magazines and newspapers that were probably unknown in the countryside. Some joined lending libraries or literary circles that offered intellectual stimulation. The city's clothing and dry goods stores put those in their home towns to shame. A wide array of Protestant churches offered Sabbath services, Sunday schools, and various social activities. Lowell offered its women workers experiences they could never have known on the farm.

Opportunities like these were dearly won. For their newfound independence, the women were required to stay for at least a year. Their working conditions were hardly healthful. The need to stand all day took its toll. To maintain humidity (necessary to keep the yarn from breaking) the windows were nailed shut, leaving the air filled with lint and making the work rooms hot, damp, and noisy. These conditions left the workers susceptible to lung disease and typhus. The boardinghouses, while certainly an improvement over the living conditions of the typical English textile worker, were crowded and ill-ventilated.

Moreover, the lives of Lowell's female workers were strictly regulated: first, by their hours of work; second, by company rules. In the 1830s the women worked long hours every day except Sunday. The workday was longest in summer, when operatives stayed at their machines for 14 hours, with brief breaks for breakfast and dinner. Hours were shorter in winter. Even then, the operatives worked by oil lamp after sunset, a practice which struck many of the young farm women as contrary to nature. True, farm work was also long and laborious, but the routines of a farm day were looser and more adaptable to human needs.

The factory bells dominated daily life. They woke the workers at 4:30 a.m. on summer mornings, called them into the mills at 4:50, rang them out for breakfast and back in, out and in for dinner, out again at 7 p.m. at the day's close. At 10 the bells rang the curfew. The mills had identical schedules and set their bells to ring in unison. The whole city, it seemed, moved together and did the mills' bidding. To a character in a story in *The Lowell Offering*, it was torment: "Up before day, at the clang of the bell—and out of the mill by the clang of the bell—into the mill, and at work, to the obedience of that ding-dong of the bell—just as though we were so many living machines."

The company also regulated the womens' conduct outside the mills. For women who did not live with relatives, residence in company board-inghouses was compulsory. Regulations posted by all the firms required boardinghouse keepers to report improper conduct to managers. Regular church attendance was expected. For a brief time the Merrimack Company even deducted pew rent from employees' earnings, paying the funds to St. Anne's, the Episcopal church built by Kirk Boott on company land. Though regulation in practice was never quite as harsh as it appeared in print, managers adopted a strict paternalism they assumed was needed to control the newly independent women. They constructed a social system acceptable to a rural public often antagonistic to urban life, thereby protecting Lowell's reputation and assuring a steady stream of new recruits into the mills.

While management sought to control mill operatives, experienced women workers had an important role in socializing newcomers, creating solidarity and a measure of freedom in the workplace. Overseers assigned novices to work alongside old hands. Only after two or three months as a "sparehand" did a new worker begin to work at her own machines. In the boardinghouses, oldtimers poked fun at the rural accents and clothing of women fresh from the farm, and they soon taught the country women the "city way of speaking." Nor did it take long for the newcomers to trade their farm clothing for more stylish urban fashions. Women helped one another adapt to a new way of life, shaping a close-knit community that formed the basis for subsequent labor organization and protest.

Background Photo:
WEAVE ROOM WORKERS, C. 1910.
Boott Cotton Mills.
Courtesy of Lowell National Historical Park.

A MILL GIRLS' LETTER

"There was not much leisure time left after the thirteen hour workday. In the few hours between supper and the ten o'clock curfew, there was the sewing of new clothes and repairing of old ones, books and magazines to read, letters to be written." [4]

TIME TABLE OF THE LOWELL MILLS,

Arranged to make the working time throughout the year average 11 hours per day.

TO TAKE EFFECT SEPTEMBER 21st., 1853.

The Standard time being that of the meridian of Lowell, as shown by the Regulator Clock of AMOS SANBORN, Post Office Corner, Central Street.

From March 20th to September 19th, inclusive.

COMMENCE WORK, at 6.30 A. M.   LEAVE OFF WORK, at 6.30 P. M., except on Saturday Evenings.
BREAKFAST at 6 A. M.   DINNER, at 12 M.   Commence Work, after dinner, 12.45 P. M.

From September 20th to March 19th, inclusive.

COMMENCE WORK at 7.00 A. M.   LEAVE OFF WORK, at 7.00 P. M., except on Saturday Evenings.
BREAKFAST at 6.30 A. M.   DINNER, at 12.30 P.M.   Commence Work, after dinner, 1.15 P. M.

BELLS.

From March 20th to September 19th, inclusive.

Morning Bells.	*Dinner Bells.*	*Evening Bells.*
First bell,..........4.30 A. M.	Ring out,.............12.00 M.	Ring out,...........6.30 P. M.
Second, 5.30 A. M.; Third, 6.20.	Ring in,...........12.35 P. M.	Except on Saturday Evenings.

From September 20th to March 19th, inclusive.

Morning Bells.	*Dinner Bells.*	*Evening Bells.*
First bell,..........5.00 A. M.	Ring out,...........12.30 P. M.	Ring out at...........7.00 P. M.
Second, 6.00 A. M.; Third, 6.50.	Ring in,.............1.05 P. M.	Except on Saturday Evenings.

SATURDAY EVENING BELLS.

During APRIL, MAY, JUNE, JULY, and AUGUST, Ring Out, at 6.00 P. M.
The remaining Saturday Evenings in the year, ring out as follows :

SEPTEMBER.		**NOVEMBER.**		**JANUARY.**	
First Saturday, ring out 6.00 P. M.		Third Saturday ring out 4.00 P. M.		Third Saturday, ring out 4.25 P. M.	
Second " " 5.45 "		Fourth " " 3.55 "		Fourth " " 4.35 "	
Third " " 5.30 "					
Fourth " " 5.20 "		**DECEMBER.**		**FEBRUARY.**	
OCTOBER.		First Saturday, ring out 3.50 P. M.		First Saturday, ring out 4.45 P. M.	
First Saturday, ring out 5.05 P.M.		Second " " 3.55 "		Second " " 4.55 "	
Second " " 4.55 "		Third " " 3.55 "		Third " " 5.00 "	
Third " " 4.45 "		Fourth " " 4.00 "		Fourth " " 5.10 "	
Fourth " " 4.35 "		Fifth " " 4.00 "			
Fifth " " 4.25 "				**MARCH.**	
				First Saturday, ring out 5.25 P. M.	
NOVEMBER.		**JANUARY.**		Second " " 5.30 "	
First Saturday, ring out 4.15 P. M.		First Saturday, ring out 4.10 P. M.		Third " " 5.35 "	
Second ". " 4.05 "		Second " " 4.15 "		Fourth " " 5.45 "	

YARD GATES will be opened at the first stroke of the bells for entering or leaving the Mills.

SPEED GATES commence hoisting three minutes before commencing work.

Penhallow, Printer, Wyman's Exchange, 28 Merrimack St.

TIME TABLE FOR THE LOWELL MILLS, 1853.

(Probably Lowell Manufacturing Company,

makers of worsted yarns and carpets).

Courtesy of the American Textile History Museum

Workdays lasted from dawn to dusk with breaks only for quick meals. For farm girls who were accustomed to working the land by the hours of daylight, the regimentation of time was a drastic transformation of their way of life. A young Vermont girl, Sarah Rice, went to work at the Masonville Cotton factory in 1845 when she was nineteen. She wrote home:

"To be sure it is a noisy place and we are confined more than I like to be. I do not wear out my clothes and shoes as I do when I do housework. If I can make two dollars per week besides my board and save my clothes and shoes I think it will be better than to do housework for nine shillings. I mean for a year or two. I should not want to spend my days in a mill unless they are short because I like a farm too well for that." [5]

Sarah Rice was typical of the early workers. She had left her family farm in order to earn some extra money with every intention of returning home. Many girls wrote of hard work, but also added that they were happy and looking forward to the end of their stay in the mills.

FREEDOM...AT A COST

The newfound freedoms enjoyed by the mill girls came with a price: lack of privacy and free time. The boardinghouse system was a strict one, with stringent rules and regulations.

REGULATIONS

FOR THE
BOARDING HOUSES
OF THE
MIDDLESEX COMPANY.

THE tenants of the Boarding Houses are not to board, or permit any part of their houses to be occupied by any person except those in the employ of the Company.

They will be considered answerable for any improper conduct in their houses, and are not to permit their boarders to have company at unseasonable hours.

The doors must be closed at ten o'clock in the evening, and no one admitted after that time without some reasonable excuse.

The keepers of the Boarding Houses must give an account of the number, names, and employment of their boarders, when required; and report the names of such as are guilty of any improper conduct, or are not in the regular habit of attending public worship.

The buildings and yards about them must be kept clean and in good order, and if they are injured otherwise than from ordinary use, all necessary repairs will be made, and charged to the occupant.

It is indispensable that all persons in the employ of the Middlesex Company should be vaccinated who have not been, as also the families with whom they board; which will be done at the expense of the Company.

SAMUEL LAWRENCE, Agent.

JOEL TAYLOR, PRINTER, Daily Courier Office.

BOARDINGHOUSE RULES
AND REGULATIONS.
*Courtesy of University of
Massachusetts, Lowell.*

A RECONSTRUCTED BOARDINGHOUSE BEDROOM IN
THE PATRICK J. MOGAN CULTURAL CENTER.
This photo depicts a bedroom usually occupied
by four women.
Photo by James Higgins.

Each small bedroom in a typical boardinghouse housed up to eight women, with two to a bed. In a story published in *The Lowell Offering*, a company-subsidized journal written by women workers, a young woman anticipates her reaction on seeing a boardinghouse:

"She thought as she looked upon the spacious, convenient chamber in which she was sitting, how hard it would be to have no place to which she could retire and be alone, and how difficult it would be to keep her things in order in the fourth part of a small apartment, and how possible it was that she might have unpleasant roommates..." [6]

EMPLOYEES IN THE
BOOTT MILLS COURTYARD, C. 1880.
Courtesy of the Lowell Historical Society.

Protest came to Lowell in the mid-1830s, only a decade after the first mill opened. Mill management, feeling for the first time the pressure of a competitive market, twice reduced the take-home pay of women workers. Faced with growing inventories and falling prices, owners believed the only way to sustain profits was to cut labor costs. The mill workers, however, were not willing to accept this logic of the marketplace.

In February 1834, after mill agents announced an upcoming wage reduction, a large group of women threatened to quit the mills if wages were cut. The agents considered it presumptuous, even "bold," for women to make such demands. When one agent dismissed a ringleader, other women followed her out of the mills and marched in a procession about the city…Though more than 800 women joined the "turn-out," the mill agents held fast. Within a couple of days most of the strikers returned to work.

Taken together, the two turn-outs reveal the Yankee women's pride and independence—qualities that made them sensitive to actions they found exploitative. As "daughters of freemen" steeped in a revolutionary tradition, they were prepared to defend themselves against the harsh economic practices of the mill owners. They did so even though they could be dismissed for striking. Those dismissed had no chance of being employed by other mills, because management circulated the names of troublemaking operatives in a blacklist.

The mill girls learned from the failure of the 1834 strike, and in the successful strike of 1836 mill workers organized to disable the factories. In reaction to a proposed increase in costs of the boardinghouses, workers strategically left their jobs to stop cloth production. Women also emptied their accounts from the banks that were associated with the Cooperatives such as the Lowell Institution for Savings.

Another period of labor unrest came in the 1840s when Lowell women, joined by other workers across New England, demanded a reduction of hours. Organizing the Lowell Female Labor Reform Association (LFLRA), with mill worker Sarah Bagley as president, they petitioned the state legislature for a ten-hour day. One of the petitions read: "We, the undersigned peaceable, industrious, hardworking men and women of Lowell…toiling from thirteen to fourteen hours per day, confined in unhealthy apartments, exposed to the poisonous contagion of air vegetable, animal, and mineral properties, debarred from proper Physical exercise, time for Mental discipline, and Mastication cruelly limited; and thereby hastening us on through pain, disease, and privation, down to a premature grave…seek a redress of those evils."

Other developments in the mills quietly transformed both work and the mill workforce. Responding to competition from new mills—often financed with profits earned in Lowell—the agents required workers to operate additional looms and spindles. They also stepped up the machines' speed: each woman now found herself trying to keep up with more machines, each one running faster. Most despised of the agents' moves was the "premium" system, in which they paid bonuses to overseers who got their workers to produce more cloth than normal.

As some Yankee women responded to these conditions by demanding reduced hours of labor, others voted silently with their feet, leaving the mills. A growing migration from the region to the Midwest left fewer native-born women to replace them on the factory floor. Mill agents were forced to look elsewhere for workers. They found their new labor supply in the Irish immigrants who, after 1845, gradually took the place of Yankee women in Lowell's labor force. The entry of immigrant workers marked the end of an era in Lowell's history and presaged a broader transformation of work and community life in the nation's leading textile city in the second half of the nineteenth century.

Pages 12, 13, 16, and 17 and portions of 14 and 15 were reprinted from Thomas Dublin, *Lowell: The Story of an Industrial City* (Lowell, MA, 1992: National Park Service), pages 40, 50-53, 55-56, 58-61. Reprinted courtesy of the Lowell National Historic Park.

[1] Lynn A. Bonfield, *"Diaries of New England Quilters Before 1860"* (Uncoverings, 1988) ed. by Sally Garouette (Mill Valley Calif; American Quilt Study Group v. 9, 1989), p. 171-197 and Lynn A. Bonfield, *"The Production of Cloth, Clothing, and Quilts in 19th Century New England Home"* (Uncoverings, 1981) ed. by Sally Garouette (Mill Valley Calif; American Quilt Study Group v. 2, 1980), p. 77-96.

[2] Gary Kulik, Roger Park, and Theodore Z. Penn, *The New England Mill Village*, 1790-1860 (Cambridge: MIT Press, 1982), intro. p.XXIV.

[3] Bernice Selden, *The Mill Girls: Lucy Larcom, Harriet Hanson Robinson, Sarah G. Bagley*. (New York: Anthaneum, 1983), p. 17.

[4] Ibid.

[5] Hazelton Rice Papers, Vermont Historical Society, Montpelier, Vermont.

[6] Benita Eisler, *The Lowell Offering: Writings by New England Mill Women 1840 - 1845* (Philadelphia: J.P. Lippencott, 1977), p. 179.

Background Photo:
THE BOBBIN GIRL, C. 1871.
Engraving by Winslow Homer.

VOICES OF THE MILL GIRLS

The mill girls had easy access to printed cottons, so why doesn't there exist a strong legacy of quilts made by Lowell's working women? It would reason that these women had neither space, time, nor the desire to make quilts during their stay in Lowell.

For most of the mill girls, precious free time was spent enjoying the social and cultural opportunities of the city. This generation of women was the first to discover real economic independence, and they delighted in both enriching their minds and spending their hard-earned money on themselves.

Frontispiece, THE LOWELL OFFERING, a literary magazine written and edited by Lowell's mill operatives, 1845.

Courtesy of the Lowell National Historical Park.

"*Is Saul also among the prophets?*"

A REPOSITORY
OF ORIGINAL ARTICLES, WRITTEN BY
"FACTORY GIRLS."

LOWELL: MISSES CURTIS & FARLEY.
BOSTON: JORDAN & WILEY, 121
Washington street.
1845.

Once in Lowell, the young women met others like themselves—proud independent daughters of Yankee farmers who were hard-working, educated, and eager to get the most out of the world. Much is known about the mill girls through their letters, and many contributed to literary publications such as *The Lowell Offering* and the more radical *Voice of Industry*...both of which contained a variety of fictional and nonfictional articles.

A representative account of life as a mill girl is portrayed in the writings of Susan Brown from Epsom, New Hampshire, who kept a diary in 1843 while she was a weaver in the Middlesex Mills.[1] Susan's diary, which she kept almost on a daily basis, rarely mentions mill work. During her stay in Lowell, Susan attended twenty-five lectures and cultural events, as well as half a dozen parties. On Sundays, her day off, she went to church, often one parish in the morning and another in the afternoon.

Susan mentions textiles often, purchasing fabric for clothing ten times. On July 10 she bought a calico dress, and on September 3, she and a friend went to dressmaker Harriet M. Blanchard's on Merrimack Street. A diary entry on September 13 states, *"Took my dress from Miss Pollards. Paid 30 cts. for cutting."* [2] It seems as if Susan often paid for having her clothes partially or completely made, since she specifies sewing only twice. In her year-long diary, there is one possible reference to quiltmaking. Two days after she went to the dressmaker's on September 5, the entry says *"...Called & left the Rose of Sharon at Mrs. Hams..."* Susan had already called on Mrs. Hams twice that week on September 2 and 4.[3] The Rose of Sharon is a documented quilt pattern, and it is possible that Susan had taken the quilt top to be finished.

Susan Brown's experience in Lowell was typical, and the large body of writing left by the mill girls indicates that their experience was urban, social, and intellectual, but not domestic. Lowell's mill girls enjoyed taking advantage of all the city's attractions before entering into married life.

HARRIET HANSON ROBINSON.

Courtesy of Boston Public Library.

A former mill girl herself, author Harriet Hanson Robinson captured the spirit of the mill girls when she wrote: "[Mill girls] could earn money and spend it as they pleased; and could gratify their tastes and desires without restraint, and without rendering an account to anyone... For the first time in this country women's labor had a value." [4]

VIEW OF MERRIMAC STREET, LOWELL, SATURDAY, AUGUST 9, 1856.

Courtesy of Lowell Historical Society.

LUCY LARCOM

"Country girls were naturally independent and the feelings that at this new work the few hours they had of every day leisure were entirely their own was a satisfaction to them. They preferred it to going out as 'hired help.' It was like a young man's pleasure in entering upon business for himself." [7]

Lucy Larcom, the best-known mill girl of the period, left her rural home in Beverly, Massachusetts, to work in the mills after her father died. Her mother opened a boardinghouse, and the eleven-year-old Lucy started work as a "doffer," changing bobbins on spinning frames. As dictated by law, she attended school for three months of the year until she turned thirteen, when she went to work full time. Lucy was initially disappointed when she had to give up school. She had dreamed of becoming a teacher, but became the most famous mill girl writer instead.

Lucy's job as a mill worker made her feel proud because she was contributing to the economic prosperity of the country as well as expanding her intellectual and social horizons. Lucy observed:

"I found that I enjoyed even the familiar unremitting clatter of the mill, because it indicated that something was going on. I liked to feel the people around me, even those whom I did not know...I felt that I belonged to the world, that there was something for me to do in it, though I had not yet found out what. Something to do; it might be very little but still it would be my own work." [5]

For these young women who were accustomed to farm work, working in the mills could be compared to a boarding school experience. The solidarity of shared experience and the notion of sisterhood developed among the mill workers, and working in Lowell often empowered them to pursue successful careers in literature, education, politics, and religion.

Lucy Larcom's writings contain much more information about her tenure in the mills than about her time spent sewing, but it seems her experience with textiles is typical of the period. She wrote:

"...it was one of my earliest accomplishments of my infancy to thread my poor, half-blind Aunt Stanley's needles for her...Many an hour I sat by her side drawing a needle and thread through a bit of calico, under the delusion that I was sewing." [6]

Sewing was not Lucy's favorite activity, but one that was part of her feminine repertoire of skills. All girls were taught to sew at a young age as an essential part of their female education and presumably most women used these skills frequently. References to sewing among the writings of the mill girls are primarily to the making and mending of clothing.

Lucy mentions quilts in her autobiography while reminiscing about how young ladies were taught at school to make quilts for their trousseau. Lucy's warm recollection of a quilt her sister made fits in well with the romanticized notion of quiltmaking after mid-century. When the Yankee farmers' daughters began working, quiltmaking was still primarily an elite activity, but by the 1840s it was encouraged as a suitable pastime for women of the middle classes who ideally had both money and time to create decorative textiles.

Ironically, while the mill girls labored thirteen-hour days, the notion of the cult of domesticity in American culture was underway. In the face of rapid industrialization, traditional roles and values were challenged. There was a sense that the world was too turbulent for women, who were needed at home to ground the family. Home was a sanctuary from modernization, and domesticity was seen as sacred. The central notion of domesticity was the contrast between home and the outside world, and it was contrary to the work values embraced by Lowell's mill girls.

As young mill workers wrote about their liberating experiences in Lowell, magazines and books dedicated to promoting a very different view of women became available to a wide audience. The most influential magazine dedicated to women's interests was *Godey's Lady's Book,* which began publication in 1837. Sarah Joseph Hale was the magazine's editor, and she often wrote advice columns to encourage her readers to serve as examples of moral behavior, as caretakers of the home and as educators of children. True women were seen as graceful, sentimental, and spiritual, but too fragile to be integrated into the male world. Hale did not regard the mill girls as appropriate young ladies, and attacked them for trying to dress above their class when she observed that:

"Many of the factory girls wear gold watches in imitation at least of all the ornaments which grace the daughters of our most opulent citizens." [8]

The mill girls, who saw themselves as embodying America's strongest values, took offense at Hale's accusation of inappropriate social climbing. A reply by a mill girl in *The Lowell Offering* rebutted with:

"Those who do not labor for their living, have more time for the improvement of their minds, for the cultivation of conversational powers, and graceful manners; but if, with these advantages, they still need richer dress to distinguish them from us, the fault must be their own, and they should at least learn to honor, merit and acknowledge talent wherever they see it." [9]

YOUNG MILL WORKERS, C. 1860.
Courtesy of the American Textile History Museum

GOLD WATCHES

"I pity the girl who cannot take pleasure in wearing the new and beautiful bonnet which her father has presented her, because, forsooth, she sees that some factory girl has, with her hard-won earnings, procured one just like it." [10]

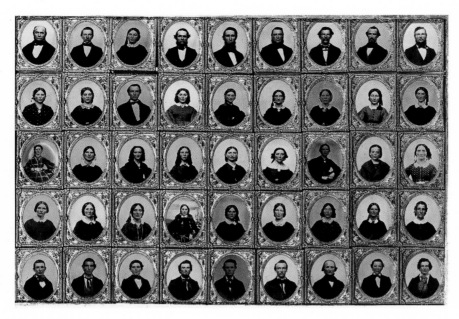

AMOSKEAG OPERATIVES, 1854.

Courtesy of the Manchester, New Hampshire, Historic Association.

Being able to afford nice clothes was a matter of pride for the mill girls, one that symbolized their newfound independence. Competition for fashionable clothing among the girls was high. Pocket money often went to the purchase of bonnets and new fabric for dresses from shops in the mill city which were stocked with the latest items.

The working girls felt that they had earned their place in the world and were contributing as much as women who kept a household. Lucy Larcom offered her more radical view of the conflict between work and womanhood:

"We may as well acknowledge that one of the unworthy tendencies of womankind is towards petty estimates of other women. If we must classify our sisters, let us broaden ourselves by making large classifications. We might all place ourselves in two ranks—the women who do something, and the women who do nothing; the first being the only creditable place to occupy." [11]

The Yankee pride and solidarity among women that empowered them to speak out against Hale's criticism also empowered them to protest against the mill owners when conditions worsened. As time progressed, the mills changed, and the labor experience that had transformed many women's lives was over. The Yankee girls moved away, on to other places and professions. The great mill girl "experiment" was no longer necessary with the advance of the industrial age.

"To be able to earn one's own living by laboring with the hands should be reckoned among female accomplishments; and I hope the time is not far distant when none of my countrywomen will be ashamed to have it known that they are better versed in useful than they are in ornamental accomplishments." [12]

[1] Mary H. Blewett, ed.; *Caught Between Two Worlds: The Diary of Lowell Mill Girl Susan Brown of Epsom, New Hampshire,* (Lowell: Lowell Museum), 1984.

[2] Ibid, p. 62.

[3] Ibid, p. 60.

[4] Jo Anne Preston, *"Millgirl Narratives: Representations of Class and Gender in Nineteenth-Century Lowell,"* Life Stories, (vol. 3, 1987), p. 27.

[5] Lucy Larcom, *A New England Girlhood Outlined from Memory* (Williamstown, Mass.: Corner House, 1889), p. 193.

[6] Ibid, p. 28.

[7] Ibid, p. 199.

[8] Benita Eisler, *he Lowell Offering: Writings by New England Women 1840-1845,* (Philadelphia: J.P. Lippencourt, 1977), p. 184.

[9] Ibid, p. 186.

[10] Ibid.

[11] Lucy Larcom, *A New England Girlhood Outlined from Memory,* (Williamstown: Corner House, 1889), p. 202.

[12] Caroline Bean, *"Dignity of Labor," The Lowell Offering,* (Series II vol 2, 1842), p. 192.

THERESA MELLO: MILL GIRL AND QUILTMAKER

Both the nature of labor and the labor force in Lowell had been transformed by the time a young Theresa Oliver emigrated from Portugal in 1892 to work as a weaver in the Boott Cotton Mills. Between 1865 and 1900 the influx of 14,000,000 immigrants flooded the factory towns.[1] Employers had much more power and control over the immigrants than they once had over the strong-willed Yankee girls. Voices of protest that had fought and won the Ten Hour Movement in the early strikes of the 1840s were no longer heard, for the immigrants were willing to work longer hours for less money, and were reluctant to organize and strike. The social structure of the workplace also changed as foreign-born men and children were increasingly employed. Unlike the one to three years the previous generation of mill girls worked, immigrant families spent their lives toiling in the mills.

"Of almost all great men, a biography has been written. Their lives and positions were such that caused them to become very prominent. However, this little sketch is about one of God's humble creatures. Her name never adorned the front page of any newspaper. Yet, she fought battles, conquered foes, and brought joy and happiness to the little sphere in which she moved. She was my mother."

Amelia Frances Mello

SAUNDERS MARKET, C. 1900. From the family of Amelia Mello Keating.

Collection of Anne and Jane Keating.

The first generation of mill workers came to the mills partially out of necessity, but mainly by choice and for personal betterment; the immigrants came for necessity alone. No longer was there a community of young women with shared experiences governed by the laws of the Cooperatives. The moralizing aspect of mill work was lost, and tenement buildings and squalid conditions began to characterize factory life.

Although Lowell's immigrants came from all over the world, they still had much in common. Most had left their homes because of hardships in their country of origin. After a grueling voyage to America they settled with a relative who arranged for them to get a job at one of the city's many mills or factories. They shared a hope for a better life and a brighter future for their children. Like the Yankee mill girls, the immigrant mill workers came primarily from agricultural worlds and had to adjust to the regimentation of time imposed by factory work. They also had to balance two cultures: that of their homeland and that of their neighborhood.

Theresa Oliver was born on the island of St. George in the Azores in 1875, the third child of John and Mary (Bettencourt) Oliver. Her family moved to Provincetown, Massachusetts when she was seventeen years old. Shortly afterwards Theresa moved to Lowell, where she lived with a married sister who secured her a job at the Boott Cotton Mills. Theresa worked her way up to weaver and tended twelve looms.

Theresa met and married Frank F. Mello, an American citizen who was originally from Terceira in the Azores. Theresa and Frank had two children, Amelia and Americo. The Mellos lived on the top floor of a triple-decker in Saunders Block, which also housed Saunders Market on the ground floor. This block was in the heart of the Portuguese community. Theresa's husband, Frank, was at one time a foreman at the James A. Thompson box factory, which made boxes to encase upright pianos. During World War I, the factory made boxes for rifles.

Theresa's life was like that of many immigrants in Lowell. She spent her life working in the mills and socializing within the Portuguese community. Theresa's knowledge of both Portuguese and English provided an important service to her community. She was respected for her skills as an interpreter, and was known for her compassion toward the sick and needy.

The first generation of Portuguese women who came to America are remembered by their daughters and granddaughters for their sewing skills and beautiful handwork. These women excelled at traditional Portuguese decorative arts such as lace making and practiced American sewing techniques such as quiltmaking and outline embroidery. Theresa Mello had an artist's eye and was a skilled needlewoman who decorated her home with embellished textiles. Much of Theresa Mello's handwork survives: lace table runners, dickeys for her clothing, and a beautiful vestment for her son Americo, who was an altar boy at St. Peter's Church.

EXTERIOR OF THE BOOTT COTTON MILLS BLDG. #6, C. 1915.
Theresa Mello is in the second row, third from the right with fellow millworkers.
From the family of Amelia Mello Keating.
Collection of Anne and Jane Keating.

Theresa also made a series of utilitarian quilts with fabrics readily available at the mills. Her work includes a dozen wool quilts in the Log Cabin Barn Raising setting and eight surviving cotton quilts in simple one-patch patterns. These scrap quilts are all tied using a wool floss. The Log Cabin quilts are made from the bright wools produced in the Middlesex mills. Many of the cottons in the one-patch quilts, especially the shirtings and delicate indigo and white prints, are typical of those made in the Merrimack mills.

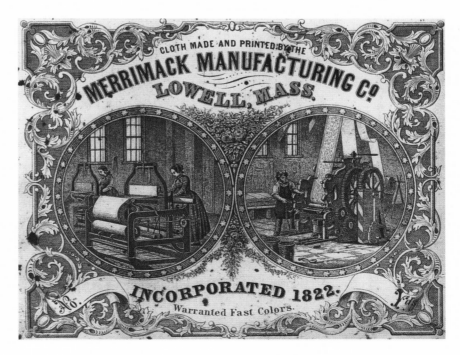

CLOTH MADE AND PRINTED BY THE MERRIMACK MANUFACTURING CO. LOWELL, MASS. INCORPORATED 1822. Warranted Fast Colors.

FABRIC LABEL FROM MERRIMACK MANUFACTURING COMPANY.
Courtesy of University of Massachesetts, Lowell.

Perhaps Theresa purchased fabric remnants prepackaged from factory stores, or friends might have taken scraps from the mill floors and brought them home to Theresa. Her quilts would not appeal to the Yankee mill girls; they are bulky, the patterns are too simple, and they contain none of the fine hand quilting that was the pride of New England quiltmakers.

Theresa worked in the mills until the birth of her children, then returned to work when Amelia and Americo were old enough for school. In 1921 she injured herself at work while lifting a bundle of heavy canvas. Theresa never recovered from the accident. She died shortly afterward and was buried at St. Patrick's Cemetery in Lowell. Theresa's granddaughters, Anne and Jane Keating, have many happy memories of her and other Portuguese ladies, all of whom were so amiable and so skilled at sewing and needle craft. They also remember accompanying their mother Amelia to the Lowell Institution for Savings, the building that is now the New England Quilt Museum.

[1] Herbert G., Gutman, ed., *Who Built America? Working People and the Nation's Economy, Politics, Culture, and Society* 2 vols. (New York: Pantheon Books, 1989), p. 267.

THERESA MELLO'S QUILTS IN BOOTT
COTTON MILLS MUSEUM.
Quilt pattern names,
left to right (all c. 1910):
Barn Raising Log Cabin, 73" x 78"
Four Patch, 70 ½" x 82"
Z-Lightning, 90 ½" x 76 ½"
New Hour Glass, 74" x 90"
Photo by James Higgins.

INTERIOR OF THE BOOTT COTTON MILLS.

Photo by James Higgins.

Pre-Industrial Quilts

The upper classes in colonial New England both appreciated fine imported goods and had the means to buy them. Between 1650 and 1850 thousands of yards of fabric were used in bed hangings alone. The bed was an ideal place to display these fine imports. It was a measure of a family's wealth, one of their most expensive possessions that was displayed prominently within the home. Typically, a high four-poster bed was draped with curtains for warmth and privacy. Quilts were made large and wide to accommodate these grand beds, which often measured roughly eight feet square. The first mention of a quilt in United States history comes from Samuel Fuller's inventory records of 1633. Among his possessions it lists a "fflock bed quilt" (the word flock referring to unspinnable tufts of coarse wool).[1] Fuller's quilt was probably made in England and brought over with his family. Wool quilts in imitation of those in European high style are the earliest American quilts.

INDIGO WORSTED WOOL, 1831.
Anonymous, initials "LB" quilted in top border, 103 ½" x 99 ½", wool, hand quilted.
Gift of The Binney Family, 1991.03.

"All wool and a yard wide" is an old New England saying denoting quality. The fronts of wool quilts were made of fine imported fabrics, while the backs were made of hand-spun, hand-loomed, and home-dyed fabrics. The bright colors in wool quilts came from natural dyes. The favorite in New England was indigo blue, as popular for its ability to hide soil as for its rich color. The wool was often glazed, making these quilts look all the richer in the flickering candlelight. Whole-cloth quilts depended on fine hand-quilted stitches for their intricate designs of feathers, wreaths, plumes, and flowers.

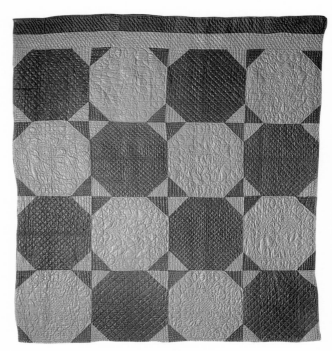

BROWN AND ROSE GLAZED SNOWBALL, C. 1800.
Mrs. Nathaniel Head, Pembroke, New Hampshire, 88 ½" x 95 ½", wool, hand pieced and quilted.
Gift of Mrs. Paul Cummings, 1989.04.

Wool quilts were popular until the 1840s, when cotton became the preferred fabric. Cotton was softer, more easily laundered and quilted, and less attractive to moths.

In New England's rural states, however, wool quilts remained in vogue throughout the entire nineteenth century due to their warmth.

CANDLEWICK SUMMER SPREAD, C. 1830.
84 ½" x 90 ½", cotton,
hand embroidered and hand tufted.
Gift of The Binney Family, 1991.04.

The candlewick spread was another type of all-white bedcover produced during the federal era. These delicate spreads were embroidered with French knots, some of which were left exposed and trimmed to form raised patterns; the fluffy dots create a look similar to that of today's chenille spreads. This technique was called "candlewicking" because the soft white cording, or roving, resembles the wicks of candles. Candlewick spreads and the Jacquard weavings of the period share much of the same imagery. The patriotic eagle is a common motif.

DETAIL OF ALL-WHITE, 1808.
Initialed "DC" and dated at the center of the quilt. Found in Burlington, Vermont, 93" x 98", cotton, hand quilted, trapunto, cording and stipple quilting.
Gift of The Binney Family, 1991.01.

The origin of the all-white quilt is European, from Italy or England during the time of Queen Anne. White was used to represent the purity and simplicity of Roman classicism, a decorative fad inspired by the archaeological discoveries of Pompeii and Heraculaneum. All-white quilts were the ultimate in luxury and workmanship, popular among elite Bostonians while whole-cloth wool quilts were in fashion. Only the most accomplished seamstress would attempt an all-white quilt, as the unbroken field of white made needlework the focus of the piece. The quilted designs are emphasized by the use of trapunto, or stuffed work, a technique that achieves a dimensional effect by gently stuffing an area with bits of cotton.

The urn featured in this quilt was a popular symbol that originated from European neoclassical sources. Memorial urns became a common symbol in decorative arts after the death of George Washington in 1800. Images of grief were especially suited to the sentiments of fine young women, and mourning was a frequent motif in women's art.

CHINTZ QUILTS

Until the mid-nineteenth century the word "chintz" was used interchangeably with the word "calico." Calico, which got its name from the Indian town Calicut, originally referred to any fabric with one or more colors. Chintz, which is most frequently found in quilts made from 1810 to 1840, is printed with floral designs in no fewer than five colors, and is generally glazed.

Right: DETAIL OF FLOWERING TREE, CENTRAL MEDALLION, C. 1835.

Gift of Dorothy Brigham, 1987.02

FLOWERING TREE, CENTRAL MEDALLION, C. 1835.

Member of the Glover Family, Massachusetts, 105" x 109", chintz, linen, hand pieced and quilted.

Gift of Dorothy Brigham, 1987.02

This quilt shows great respect for the textiles: the design is a combination of only a few prints, and large expanses of fabric are kept whole. The two outer borders are made from an imported English chintz, while the central border, second border, and central medallion are from an eighteenth century palampore.

Prior to the seventeenth century, European taste was influenced by the great tradition of tapestry and embroidery, and woven textiles were the most popular fabrics. In the second half of the century, the East India Company in England began importing textiles from India along with other commodities such as spices. These textiles were exquisite block-printed and painted cottons known as palampores. It is thought that these spreads were sent not in trade, but as bribes or tokens of appreciation for English patrons. None of these original cottons survive, but in the 1640s British entrepreneurs began to commission palampore designs for the European market. The English loved these lightweight cottons, which became all the rage among the wealthy for furnishings and clothing. In 1687 this infatuation led to a French ban on the import of textiles from India, and from 1720 through 1736 England outlawed clothing made of printed calicoes. In response to restrictions on the coveted imports, and with the help of industrial innovation, Europeans began to make their own cotton prints. These are the chintzes that appear in early American quilts.

American quiltmakers first used chintz in whole panels. Later they cut specific motifs from the fabric and appliquéd them onto a neutral background, a technique called *broderie perse*. As the popularity of *broderie perse*—also known as cut work—grew, manufacturers printed chintzes specifically for use in quilts. These fabrics contained small motifs for the cut work, as well as large expanses of florals for use in quilt borders. Now quiltmakers could imitate the designs of expensive printed chintzes and palampores without the extravagant cost of many yards of imported fabric. The collage-like technique also gave women more freedom of artistic expression. In the federal era the decorative arts were at their height, and some of America's most beautiful quilts were made during the period.

PRINCESS CHARLOTTE COMMEMORATIVE, 1820–1840.
Anonymous, 88 ¾" x 89 ¾", chintz, cotton, hand appliquéd, pieced and quilted.
Gift of The Binney Family, 1991.13.

Chintz appliqué was popular in all the colonies; in New England, the favorite design was a medallion style with a single central motif, often with borders. The innermost medallion on this quilt is a fabric commemorating the marriage of Princess Charlotte of Wales to Prince Leopold of Saxenbourg on May 2, 1816. Commemorative textiles were popular in America and England, appearing in quilts made throughout the century.

DETAILS OF EIGHT-POINTED STAR,
C. 1820.

Gift of Irene King, 1996.07.

EIGHT-POINTED STAR, C. 1820.
Member of the Cook-Borden Family,
Fall River, Massachusetts, 104" x 109",
chintz, cottons, toiles, hand pieced,
appliquéd and quilted.

Gift of Irene King, 1996.07.

This is a fine example of an early New England
high-style quilt. Like many New England
quilts from this era, it is cut at the corners
to fit a four-poster bed. The quilt contains
a variety of luxury fabrics—linen/cottons,
toiles, cottons, and chintz prints—and is an
early example of an eight-pointed star pattern.
Its three border panels are made of chintz
printed with a pillar design, reflecting once
again the early nineteenth century fascination
with the classical world.

*Fabric was extraordinarily
expensive in colonial America.
Nevertheless, imported chintz
was highly regarded, and
often found its way into
New England diaries and
wills. Documents of the time
provide plentiful evidence of
this tendency, as in John
Adams' 1776 diary entry
describing the "rich beds with
crimson damask curtains
and counterpanes" found in
the homes of Boston's elite.*

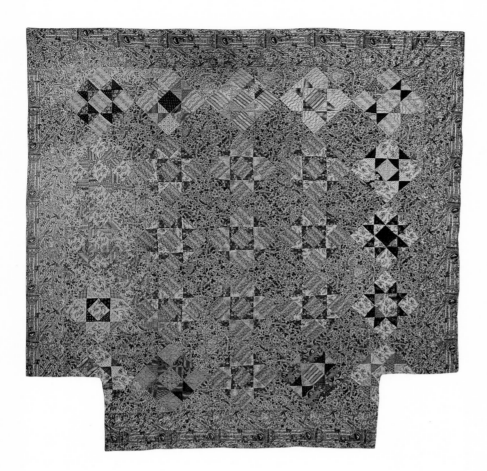

PIERCE FAMILY HOMESTEAD QUILT,
c. 1835.

Member of the Pierce Family, West Warwick,
Rhode Island, 117 ¼" x 116", chintz,
cotton, hand pieced and quilted.

Museum purchase with funds donated by the Narragansett
Bay Quilters, 1988.04. Photo by Paul Rocheleau, courtesy
of The Magazine ANTIQUES.

The quiltmaker added an elegant touch to
the otherwise simple design when she set her
variable star blocks on point, then alternated
them with solid squares of blue chintz.
The border is an English roller print of
delicate birds and butterflies surrounding a
classical pillar. This incongruous combination
of motifs is not unusual—European fabric
designers borrowed from many sources,
focusing more on visual appeal than
historical accuracy.

WOODEN AND METAL QUILTING STENCILS,
1800s.

Museum purchase, 1989.10.

Photo by Bob Paré.

These wooden stencils are wonderful examples
of the templates used to mark quilts in the
early nineteenth century. Florence Peto, an
early historian of quilts, wrote:
"Sailors from Nantucket and all along the
New England coast carved such blocks from
lightweight wood, presents for the quiltmaking
womenfolk. The quilter would dust the face of
the block with chalk and transfer the pattern
to the material."[2] The tin stencils would be
dusted and the marks left would be followed
with the needle much as one follows a
"dot to dot" pattern.

---

[1] From Plymouth, MA. Pilgrim Hall, Samuel Fuller inventory, 1633. As quoted in Nancy Halpern, *Northern Comfort: Three-Hundred-and-Fifty Years of New England Quilts*, (unpublished manuscript, 1983), p. 9.

[2] As quoted by Mrs. Florence Peto in Myron Orlofsky and Patsy Orlofsky, *Quilts in America*, (New York: McGraw Hill, 1974), p. 153-154.

THE INDUSTRIAL REVOLUTION AND BEYOND

By 1840, the Industrial Revolution had firmly established cotton production in the Northeast, which dramatically lowered the cost of textiles. The period from 1840 to 1860 was blessed by a good economy, an industrial boom, and increased leisure time to quilt. Fabrics originally available only to the wealthy became affordable to the middle classes, and quiltmaking became a much more democratic pastime.

A new type of quilt, the album or friendship quilt, was all the rage from the 1840s through the 1870s. Friendship quilts were inspired by popular autograph albums, in which young ladies collected signatures and verses. Album quilts were one of the many styles of ceremonial quilts made to commemorate going west, engagements, coming of age, marriages, and deaths. With the opening of the west and the creation of the transcontinental railway system, the nation's population had become much more mobile. In 1850, one-third of United States citizens lived

outside the state or nation in which they were born. Album blocks could be sent easily through the mail, and hundreds of these quilts were made as remembrances for friends and family moving beyond New England forever. Newly formed ladies' magazines encouraged making autograph quilts, even publishing sample verses and quotes—a favorite was "Blest be the tie that binds"—as inspiration. Because the ladies' magazines that spurred the album quilt craze were on the eastern seaboard, as their readership moved westward, the fashion did as well.

Signature quilts were not fancy; they were usually made with fabrics from the scrapbag and the quilting was neither fine nor extensive, as it served primarily as a memento. Today, these quilts are important historical documents: before 1850 only the heads of families were listed in the government census, and signature quilts provide rare records of women's lives.

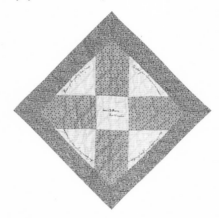

Inscribed within the central block of this quilt
is the following:

Carrie F. Foster West Henniker
Please accept this quilt, my dear friend
to atone for a loss we cannot amend
And let troubles pass by fraught with despair
And learn with a light heart life's sorrows to bear

This quilt may have commemorated the
loss of a child: Carrie had been married that
same year, and there is no record that any
of her relatives passed away.

The Autograph Cross, also known as Album Block or Chimney Sweep, was the most
common, one-block pattern used in signature quilts. A participant decorated the strip of
muslin at the center of the block by embellishing it with her name or a short verse in silk
or cotton thread. When indelible inks came on the market they facilitated the decoration
of autograph quilts with delicate signatures or elaborate hand stamping.

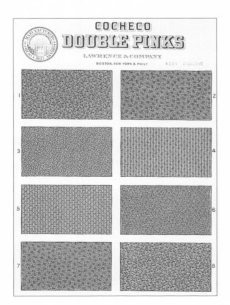

The double-pink fabrics in the quilt above
were likely produced at the Cocheco Print
Works in New Hampshire.

The Amish quilts of Lancaster County are
especially known for their bold colors.
Non-Amish quiltmakers of the region
were also fond of using saturated colors.

Streak of Lightning, like the more common
Midwestern favorite, Star of Bethlehem,
was an early example of piecing with a
45-degree diamond. This is a difficult
pattern, and without careful piecing,
the quilt top will curl.

This quilt, rich in family memories,
embodies our romantic notion of
quiltmaking. Made by Rebecca Fonk Eugle
as a wedding gift for her daughter,
Cynthia, the quilt celebrates her coming
of age and commemorates her youth.
The pink and yellow coordinating fabrics
are thought to be from childhood dresses
belonging to Cynthia and those of her
sister, Katherine.

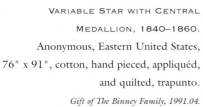

Early American quiltmaking evolved into
two distinct styles: the central medallion
and the block style, which after 1850
became the far more common of the two.
This quilt incorporates both styles, recalling
pre-industrial quilts with the prominent
central medallion and the *broderie perse*
leaves and flowers. The quiltmaker used a
variety of techniques in this piece, combining
appliqué, piecing, and trapunto.

LeMoyne Star, c. 1840.
Anonymous, Pennsylvania, 74" x 83",
cotton, hand pieced and quilted.
Gift of The Binney Family, 1991.07.

Touching Stars, c. 1850.
Anonymous, New England, 74" x 90",
cotton, hand pieced, appliquéd, and quilted.
Gift of The Binney Family, 1991.36.

The appliqué stars on this summer spread are made from the brilliant and colorfast Turkey red. From the Middle Ages to the eighteenth century, the primary red dye was madder, a brownish red made from a perennial shrub called *rubia tinctorum*. The first bright red in Europe was imported from Mexico, but the process was very expensive, requiring 70,000 cochineal beetles to make a single pound of dye.

Meanwhile, Middle Eastern dyemakers had discovered a way to make bright red from madder, but—much to the frustration of European manufacturers—they kept their process secret. Finally, in 1786 English dyer John Wilson of Manchester learned the complex series of steps to make Turkey red (named for its Middle Eastern origin). This clear, saturated, and colorfast red was used widely, but was especially popular in mid-century red and green floral quilts. Unlike many dyes, Turkey red has not faded, and is as brilliant today as it was 150 years ago.

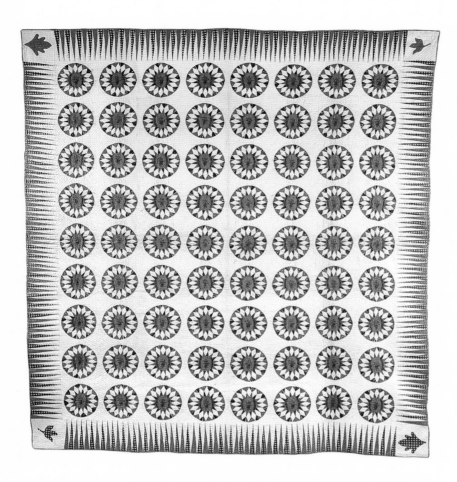

SUNBURST WITH SHARP NEEDLE
POINTED BORDER, C. 1855.
Anonymous, Greenwich, Ohio, 92" x
101 ½", cotton, hand pieced, appliquéd,
and quilted.
Gift of The Binney Family, 1991.08.

This quilt is a showcase of the maker's
skill with a needle—a complex border sets
off the already difficult Sunburst pattern.
Though many people believe that quilts
were always made from clothing scraps,
a presentation piece such as this was
meticulously planned and the fabrics
carefully selected.

LOG CABIN, C. 1865.
Sarah Bryant, Scituate, Massachusetts,
68" x 75", cotton, hand pieced and quilted.
Gift of The Binney Family, 1995.20.
Photo by Greg Heins.

Many Log Cabin quilts were made during
the latter part of the nineteenth century.
The red squares in the center of each block
are called "chimneys," and represent the
hearths central to rural homes in the
American West. The pattern was possibly
a revival, meant to evoke romantic notions
of the first homes settlers built during the
great westward migrations.

Quilts from 1850-1880 have many features in common. Floral quilts are usually appliqué, for the technique is well-suited to creating the curving vines, intricate flowers, birds, and fruits which adorn the surfaces of these pieces. Bright reds and greens were the favorite colors in these quilts.

PRINCESS FEATHER, 1850–1870.
Anonymous, 72 ½" x 73 ½", cotton,
hand appliquéd and quilted.
Gift of The Binney Family, 1991.10.

The large floral designs on this piece reflect the exaggerated forms of the Rococo period in American design (1840–1860).

APPLIQUÉD PINEAPPLE, 1860–1880.
Anonymous, Pennsylvania,
104 ½" x 104 ½", cotton, hand appliquéd and quilted with a diagonal chain design.
Gift of The Binney Family, 1991.06.

It is said that American sea captains impaled pineapples on their entry gates to announce their return from sea. The pineapple is a symbol of hospitality and goodwill that often finds its way into American decorative arts.

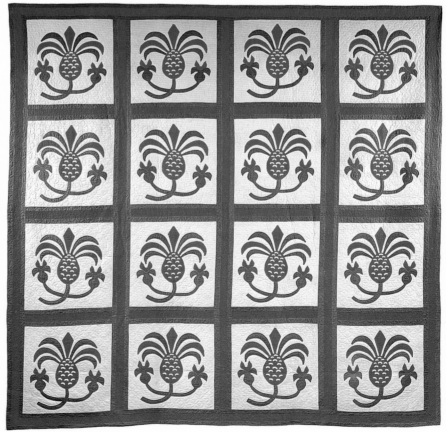

PEONY QUILT, C. 1870.
Made by either Abigail Bentley Larkin (1811–1898) or Abigail's daughter, Sarah Ann Larkin Marshall (1838-1908), Tolland, Massachusetts, 76" x 93", cotton, hand appliquéd and quilted.

Gift of Elise B. Simmons, 1988.06.

In her diary entry of March 8, 1870, Sarah Ann Larkin Marshall wrote: "At home all day quilting." From the estimated date of this quilt, however, either she or her mother, Abigail Bentley Larkin, could have been the maker. Whichever woman pieced it, the Peony pattern in this "never-used" quilt is beautifully designed and executed. In all of the squares the stems are directed away from the quilt's center, a gentle reminder that quilts were once planned only for use on beds. Flower groupings remained upright when the quilt was draped over the two sides and foot of the mattress.

CROSSED TULIPS,
QUILT TOP, 1850–1870.
Anonymous, probably Massachusetts,
87" x 86", cotton, hand appliquéd
and quilted.
Gift of Dorothy Brigham, 1987.01.

This quilt top was begun in the late
nineteenth century. It was not finished,
however, until sometime between 1950
and 1980, when Dorothy Brigham found
the top in Lynn, Massachusetts. The appliqué
design is an adaptation of one of the
many tulip patterns available to nineteenth
century quiltmakers; the red border and
red-and-white prairie points were
added when the quilt was completed
a generation later.

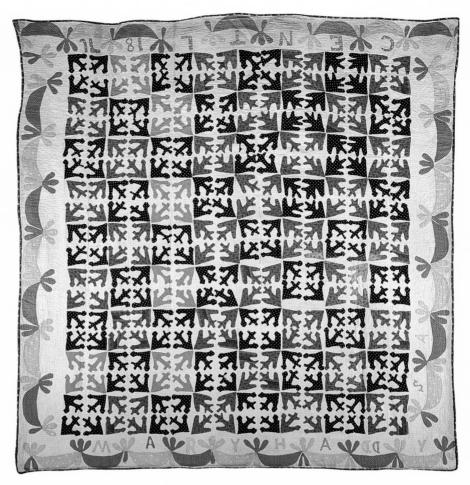

CENTENNIAL QUILT, 1876.
Mary Haddy, Cape Cod, Massachusetts?,
86" x 88", cotton, hand appliquéd and
quilted.
Gift of The Binney Family, 1991.25.

America celebrated the Centennial with
enthusiasm: it was a time to look forward
to the advances of the industrial age and
to admire the achievements of the past.
Mary Haddy's quilt is one of the many
decorative-arts pieces made to memorialize
the country's birthday. The inscription
documents her name and the date in the
borders. The appliquéd motifs are in red,
white, and blue. Fine cotton quilts like
this one were made throughout the
nineteenth century, even in the latter part
of the century, when crazy patchwork
became the favored style.

MAINE FLORAL APPLIQUÉ, C. 1850.
Anonymous, Maine, cotton, 71" x 91",
hand appliquéd and quilted.
Gift of the Burlington-Terryville Quilters Guild, 1987.05.

What makes this quilt unusual is the informality
and artistic freedom of design—a true
expression of American folk art.

MISSISSIPPI SIGNATURE QUILT TOP, 1901.
Friends and former slaves at Dixie
Plantation, Garden City, Michigan,
83 ½" x 90 ½", cotton, hand pieced
and embroidered.
Gift of Elizabeth Richter McCleary, 1988.11.

The divisions in antebellum society between
North and South and black and white are
mirrored in this quilt top, made as a farewell
gift for Cynthia Eugle Ball and A.V. Ball.

The couple moved back North after their
forty-one years on a Dixie plantation in
Mississippi. The first four rows of blocks
are the work of Northerners who visited the
St. James Hotel and Colony, which seems
to have been in some way associated with
the Dixie property. Below those blocks are
four rows signed by southern whites, and
the last four rows were signed by former
slaves at the plantation.

The inscriptions on the quilt reveal a lot
about the community who signed it.
(From the rows by northern folks):
Mrs. DeGroat, Landlady of St. James Hotel
(From rows by southern whites):
*Nellie Ball, Fred's sister, married Shep
Whitehead. So you can see the old
plantation are our folks.*
(From rows by former slaves):
*"Old Aunt E-Dee", slave of another
plantation owner.*

VICTORIAN ERA SILK QUILTS AND CRAZY QUILTS

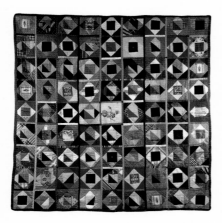

BACON SILK CRAZY, 1850-1880.
Anonymous, 72" x 70", silks and satins,
tufted.

Gift of Bessie Rilla Milne, 1984.01.

Although the title of this quilt refers to it
as a crazy quilt, it is more accurate to call
it silk patchwork. In 1850–1851, *Godey's
Lady's Book* published as a series the pattern
for a Diamond in a Square quilt to be made
with silk, and it is possible this quilt was
made shortly thereafter. Just as silk super-
seded cotton for fashionable women's
clothing, it was to become the most
popular material for stylish quilts.

BEMIS CRAZY QUILT, 1884.
Eleanor Bemis, 55 ¼" x 68 ½", silks,
satins, velvets, hand pieced and
embroidered, tufted.
Gift of Mrs. Gilliand, 1993.02.

The second half of the nineteenth century was the heyday of American quiltmaking. The Industrial Revolution provided the middle class with greater disposable income, and the development of household machinery left additional time for leisurely pursuits. For the first time, women could afford luxury materials and emulate the upper-class lifestyle. Unlike the British leisure class, who had inherited a pattern of social responsibilities to fill the days, Americans still believed in Puritan values, one of the strongest being the value of industry.

Middle-class women, no longer needing to work for money, spent their free time in feminine pursuits; one of the most highly regarded of these was the creation of household decorative arts. Many sincerely believed that the values of culture and refinement were found in material goods. During this era of rapid social change, a great deal of effort was made to emphasize women's traditional roles, and fancy needlework was considered the "most elegant of female accomplishments."

The Victorian era was characterized by a love of souvenirs that women assembled into pictorial albums and scrapbooks. In that capacity women became record keepers of American culture.

Crazy quilts also reflected the Victorians' love of mementos, acting as scrapbooks in cloth. They were a diary of the maker's life and featured treasured bits of old gowns, ribbons from political campaigns, and printed silks that often contained symbolic or sentimental meaning. Silk crazy quilts were made smaller than traditional quilts. They were also the first quilts that were primarily decorative, meant to serve more as a subject of reflection or light conversation than a utilitarian purpose.

In 1862, Queen Victoria entered mourning for the death of her beloved husband, Prince Albert. In response to Victoria's strict observance, proper society adopted similar elaborate, lengthy mourning practices. Women's social activities were restricted during these long periods, leaving time for fancywork. Many decorative arts, including crazy quilts, were made as memorials.

While crazy quilts were a descendant of paper memory-pieces in terms of content, the design had quite separate influences. The most immediate of these was a result of the 1876 Centennial Exhibition, held on the grounds of Fairmount Park in Philadelphia. Nine million Americans visited the Japanese Pavilion, and became fascinated with Japanese decorative arts. The exhibition prompted a rage to use Oriental motifs in home decor. The bold colors and asymmetrical arrangements of the Japanese aesthetic directly influenced the exotic crazy quilt designs.

Women were also inspired by the Exhibition's show of embroidered household objects from London's Royal School of Art Needlework. In 1877, Candace Wheeler founded the New York School of Decorative Arts, basing it on the British model, and the art needlework movement flourished in the United States. American women used these new embroidery stitches to enhance the surfaces of crazy quilts with elaborate designs.

"How to" books and magazines began to profoundly impact women's artistic lives. In his widely read book, *Hints on Household Taste,* Charles Eastlake urged women to use artistic furniture. Every available space was to be covered with decorative items—the more brilliant the colors and incongruous the combinations the better.

Monthly magazines for women, such as *Godey's Lady's Book,* became the arbiters of taste and social behavior. In addition to stories, social columns, and patterns, a regular feature was instructions for craft projects. Crazy quilts represented one of the ways to use fancywork. Objects such as fans, wall pockets, napkin holders, key boxes, and embroidered slippers were all made using fancywork techniques.

In the early twentieth century, popular society reacted to the material culture of the Victorian era. The elaborate objects and artifacts came to be viewed as "dust collectors" and home decor became more minimal.

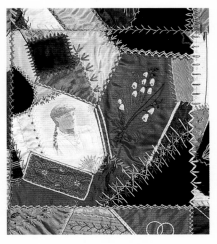

DETAIL FROM WHITE REED CRAZY QUILT.

Gift of Virginia Reed, 1986.01. Photo by Greg Heins.

Decorative textiles were an integral part of a fine home. They softened corners, muffled noise, and served as a general symbol of the civilizing influence of a diligent housewife.

SEWING TOOL DOLL AND 1865 PATTERN IN *Godey's Lady's Book.*

Gift of Virginia Mauder, 1998.04.

Photo by Bob Paré.

HEXAGONAL STAR WITH
CRAZY BORDER, 1880–1900.
Anonymous, Nantucket, Massachusetts,
51 ½" x 51 ½", silks and velvets,
hand pieced and appliquéd, embroidered.
Gift of The Binney Family, 1998.02.

LOWELL CRAZY QUILT, 1893–1904.
Blanche Wiggin Staples (Robinson), Lowell,
Massachusetts, 60" x 72", silks, satins,
taffetas, velvets, hand appliquéd, pieced,
and embroidered.
Gift of Judith Hall, 1989.02. Photo by Greg Heins.

Blanche made this quilt when she was a
young woman, probably for her trousseau.
A silk bandanna from the 1893 Chicago
World's Fair serves as the central medallion.
The quilt is balanced at the four corners by
pieces cut from a single handkerchief showing
the flags of many nations. Someone, perhaps
Blanche's mother, gave her a souvenir ribbon
from the Women's Pavilion at the Philadelphia
Centennial Exhibition, which was held the
year before Blanche was born.

The ribbon promoting Frederick T.
Greenhalge's successful Congressional
campaign may have come from her father,
who had political leanings. Both parents
were active Baptists; they probably brought
her the ribbon commemorating the 1888
Adoniram Judson Centennial at Malden's
First Baptist Church. Finally, Blanche
included a personal souvenir in her quilt, a
hand-painted ribbon reading "onze Party,
June 4, 1888, Motto, Love," which was
probably made in honor of her eleventh
birthday party. (*Onze* is French for eleven.)

*Strict social mores of
the time encouraged all
practical work to be
completed by mid-day.
The afternoons were then
spent on creating fancywork
at the embroidery frame,
or with the artist's box
painting delicate watercolors.
The romantic image of a
young woman working
daintily on a fancywork
project encouraged many
unmarried ladies to keep a
project in the embroidery
frame at all times should a
male visitor come calling.*

MOODY LUEY CRAZY QUILT, 1875.
Mary Moody Luey, Deerfield, Massachusetts, 53" x 60", ribbons, moiré, satin, silks, velvets, damasks, brocades, hand pieced and embroidered, tufted.
Gift of Mary Moody Luey Hazelton, 1992.01.

Mary Moody Luey made her crazy quilt when she was fifty-seven years old. None of the sewing was done on the Sabbath, for the Lueys were a devout family. In a letter dated 1923, Mary's daughter, Martha Ellen Luey Parish remembered, *"Have heard mother say as the sun went down Saturday night—all sewing was put down and the Saturday evening and Sunday until the sun went down were observed as holy time."*

CIGAR SILK PILLOW BACK

Cigar smoking was the favorite use of tobacco during this period, and the production of cigar silks indicates that manufacturers understood the popularity of commemorative ribbons for use in Victorian quilts. The silks for this pillow cover were collected by Agnes S. Mushet's husband Frank, who probably acquired them in the 1890s when he worked as head of concessions at the Glen Forest Amusement Park in Methuen, Massachusetts. Pillow covers were a popular way to use cigar silks, as they were smaller than traditional quilts that would have required several hundred pieces (and an abundance of cigar purchases) to complete.

WHITE REED CRAZY QUILT, 1885.
Carrie White Reed, Chelmsford,
Massachusetts, 61" x 46", velvets, silks and
satins, hand pieced and embroidered,
painting on silk, tufted.
Gift of Virginia Reed, 1986.01.
Photo by Greg Heins.

In addition to the many embroidered
pictures on this quilt (a spider and web, a
coffee cup, moons, stars, and Halley's comet
among them), Carrie White Reed included
delicate hand-painted flowers on some of
the satin pieces. Painting on fabric was a
popular pastime, and a painted motif could
save hours with the needle. Kensington
embroidery was a technique used to fill in
outlined designs on crazy patchwork, and a
method called Kensington painting, done
with a pen that deposited thick lines of paint
onto the fabric, was developed to imitate the
embroidery stitches.

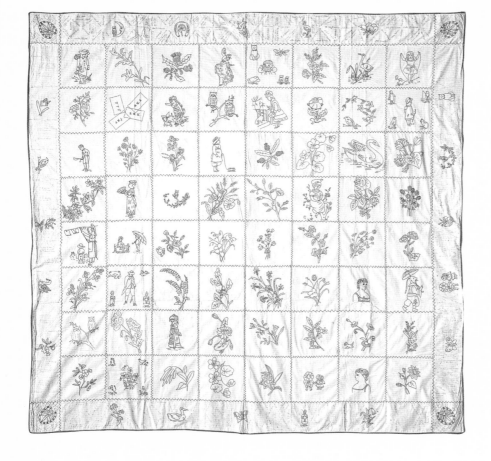

KATE GREENAWAY, 1875–1900.
Anonymous, 80" square, cotton with
embroidered figures.
Gift of Arnold Blake, 1988.10.

Embroidery's popularity enjoyed a revival
from the last quarter of the nineteenth century to the early twentieth century. Outline
embroidery, or "etching on linen", worked
primarily in one color, was used to decorate
towels, napkins, dresser scarves, and bedcovers.
Illustrations by the British children's author
Kate Greenaway, which depicted frolicking
children, pets, and flowers, became quite
popular. This quilt was probably used as a
fundraiser, as indicated by the inked signatures
on the border which include the names of
two American presidents, Benjamin Harrison
and Grover Cleveland.

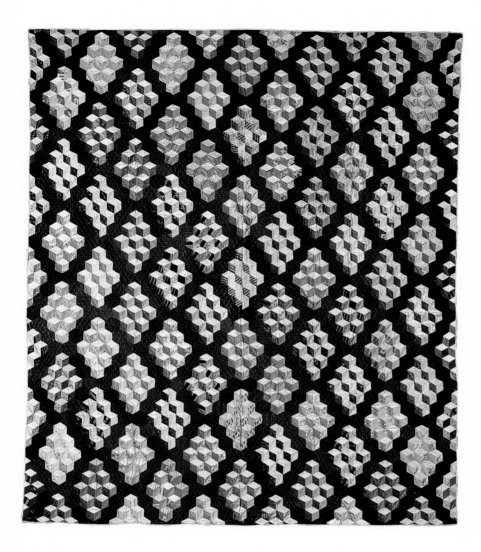

TUMBLING BLOCKS, 1880–1900.
Anonymous, 75 ½" x 90 ½",
silk, hand pieced.
Gift of The Binney Family, 1991.22.

Victorian needleworkers made pieced patterns in silks and satins without embellishments, as well as the highly decorated crazy quilts. In both, the fine materials were a sign of wealth and luxury, while the elaborate stitching on crazy quilts demonstrated a woman's devotion to industriousness. At the end of the century quiltmakers began experimenting with patterns that create optical illusions, and the Tumbling Block is one of the richest of this type. Newly perfected aniline dyes created brilliant light-reflecting silks whose rich colors emphasize the three-dimensional patterns and anticipate modern design.

Commemorative crazy quilts borrowed styles from album and other signature quilts popular earlier in the century. Members of the Ladies' Aid Society made this quilt for the Pastor George Banks Mead on his arrival to the Methodist church in North Egremont, where he served from 1886 to 1888.

MEAD CRAZY QUILT, 1886.
Members of the Ladies' Aid Society,
North Egremont, Massachusetts,
67" x 57", silk, satin, ribbons,
chenille embroidery.
Gift of Jean and Gordon Mead, 1997.03.

PASTOR GEORGE BANKS MEAD
AND HIS WIFE IDA AMELIA
TURNER MEAD.

COLONIAL REVIVAL QUILTS

PINE TREE, 1880–1900.
Anonymous, New England, 81" x 70",
cotton, hand pieced and quilted.
Gift of The Binney Family, 1991.27.

The Pine Tree is a revival quilt,
featuring several possible references to
colonial America in the design. The first
coins minted in the United States in 1652
in Massachusetts featured a pine tree image.
The design might also be an early
Massachusetts pattern known as the
Tree of Life, said to have been inspired
by the New England landscape.

DOUBLE SQUARE STAR VARIATION, C. 1860.
Anonymous, 83" x 97", cotton, hand pieced
and quilted, trapunto.
Gift of The Binney Family, 1991.29.

Blue and white quilts often contain elaborate
hand quilting and demonstrate a woman's
finest needle skills. The use of trapunto or
stuffed work is an homage to the all-white
quilts of the pre-industrial era.

The Colonial Revival became a popular decorative arts style in the decades following the Centennial. This call for the simplicity of past times was in part America's pride in her history and in part a reaction to the vibrant art of the Aesthetic Movement. Two-color quilts with intricate patterns imitated the look of woven colonial coverlets. Almost every accomplished quiltmaker made a two-color quilt; the favorite combination was blue and white. Indigo dyes, which yielded rich blues, had been favored by colonial women, and were known to be inexpensive and durable since the seventeenth century. The use of indigo-dyed fabric was as patritoic as the name given the patterns, such as Burgoyne Surrounded Variation (see page 76 for a quilt pattern). The pattern name refers to a famous battle of the American Revolution. During the 1850s the same pattern was called Rocky Road to California, referring to the great westward migrations.

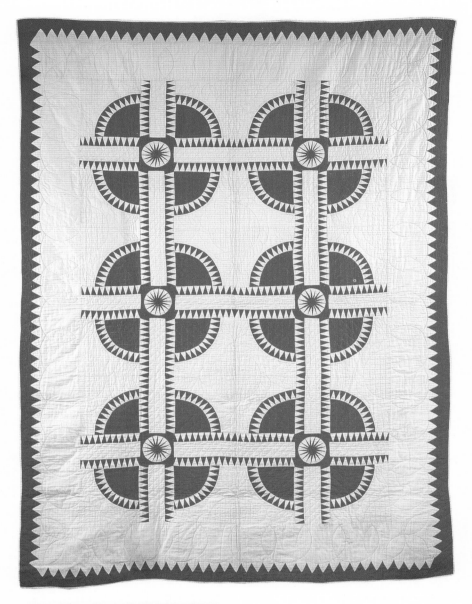

NEW YORK BEAUTY, 1870–1900.
Anonymous, Oregon, 69" x 92",
cotton, hand-pieced blocks and
machine-pieced borders.
Gift of The Binney Family, 1991.32.

Despite what the name would lead us to expect, most existing New York Beauty quilts were not made in New York. They are most frequently found in the southern states of Tennessee, Alabama, and the Carolinas. They were probably made as political quilts, called Polk in the White House, commemorating James K. Polk's election to the Presidency in 1844. Quilt historians trace the New York Beauty pattern to the 1840s, and cite as many as twenty-five different names, the most popular being Rocky Mountain, Crown of Thorns, and Sunrise. In 1930, batting manufacturer Stearns & Foster published this pattern, stating that it dated back to the colonial days; however, true colonial quilt patterns do not contain such complex piecework, and would have been made of wool, or imported chintz with *broderie perse*.

RISING SUN (OR SUNFLOWER) WITH
EAGLE BORDER, 1870–1880.
Nancy Ganong, Irontown, Michigan,
72 ½" x 99", cotton, hand pieced,
appliquéd, and quilted.
Gift of The Binney Family, 1991.26.

SCHOOLHOUSE OR OLD HOME IN A
GARDEN MAZE, 1890–1910.
Anonymous, 91" x 81", cotton,
hand pieced and quilted.
Gift of The Binney Family, 1991.11.

The rural schoolhouse is a widely recognized symbol of America's past. The painter Winslow Homer depicted children at play in front of a one-room schoolhouse in his engraved illustration, *Snap the Whip*. Published in *Harper's Weekly* in the 1870s, the image became an iconic reminder of America's idyllic past. Quilters adopted the schoolhouse image and made many variations of the pattern. This quilt is typical of its period: the repetitive blocks are constructed from cotton calico scraps, and the sashing, or "garden maze," makes the piecing difficult.

DEPRESSION ERA QUILTS

Depression-era styles often contrasted with the reality of difficult times. Depression-era quilts were made in pastel colors and art nouveau styles, with elegant borders and dreamlike, luxurious designs. Fabric was more appealing, thanks to newly available German dyes which allowed manufacturers to create a rainbow of brightly printed cottons. Decorated with whimsical scenes or bold art-deco designs, their lively visual images contrasted dramatically with the somber cottons of the Victorian era.

WATER LILY, 1938.

Katherine Willard Richter, 69 ½" x 88",
cotton, hand pieced, appliquéd, and quilted.
A tag inscribed "KWR 1938" is sewn to
the binding on the back of the quilt.
Gift of Elizabeth Richter McCleary, 1988.04.

The rapid urbanization and economic prosperity of the 1920s inspired both preservation and celebration of the country's historic and cultural past. Although the Great Depression brought hard times to America, the Works Progress Administration provided jobs for thousands, including the documentation of folk culture. Quilts were true American folk art, based on patterns and traditions handed down by families and tight-knit communities. Additionally, quilts were utilitarian, providing warmth and symbolizing a return to practical and frugal living. The quilt became a patriotic symbol of the colonial homemaker and of simple days gone by.

As quilting experienced another renaissance in the 1920s and 1930s, women became the first quilt entrepreneurs and historians. Hundreds of women participated in quilt design and production, and a new, thriving cottage industry gave a generation of women significant professional opportunities. Writers such as Ruby Short McKim, who designed patterns for the *Kansas City Star* and *Better Homes and Gardens,* and Anne Orr, who was the art needlework editor of *Good Housekeeping Magazine,* regularly published patterns and articles about quilting. A Gallup survey conducted in six large cities in 1935 showed that the quilting article was the most popular feature in Sunday papers.[1]

Quilts became easier to make as kits containing stamped or pre-cut fabrics became available through women-owned businesses. Kits came with easy-to-follow directions and all the necessary fabric, and thus standardized quilt production. The tradition of pattern exchange turned to pattern purchase; and making the same patterns available nationwide homogenized regional quiltmaking. Though many scholars dismiss kits as unoriginal, they gave artistic opportunity to those who might never have made quilts otherwise. The designs, appliqué being the favorite, were often a challenge to make. Quilting became a popular hobby, and despite all the modern tools available, most women still hand-stitched their quilts.

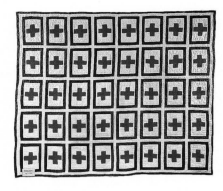

RED CROSS, 1919.
Emmy Lord, 74" x 64", cotton, hand appliquéd red crosses on white rectangles, blue border and box sashing; hand quilted with two concentric hearts in white thread in the center of each cross.
Gift of The Binney Family, 1991.33.

During the first World War, publications such as *Ladies' Home Journal* and *Harper's Bazaar* urged women to make quilts for "our boys over there." Many women answered the call, and Red Cross quilts like this one, made by Emmy Lord when she was 82 years old, were donated to aid local chapters.

FLAG SQUARES, C. 1940.
Anonymous, 90" x 75 ½", cotton, hand pieced and quilted.
Gift of The Binney Family, 1991.24.

Quilts with patriotic themes have been made since the Revolutionary War. During times of national celebration and crisis, American women express the prevailing attitudes of the country with their nationalistic quilts. Here, the American flag has been stylized to accommodate the fashion of the time. This quilt was probably made from a kit; many kits from this era contained patterns with patriotic themes.

JUVENILE PRINTS CRIB QUILT, DOUBLE
WEDDING RING, C. 1930.
Anonymous, 33" x 50", cotton, machine
pieced and appliquéd, tied with embroidery
floss, no batting.
Gift of Arnold Blake, 1988.03.

The Double Wedding Ring pattern first
became popular after the Civil War. Women
are said to have carefully collected scraps for
these treasured quilts for years. This quilt
contains an assortment of juvenile prints,
maybe taken from sample books—a possibility
suggested by the small size of the pieces and
the appearance of the same print in
several colorways.

BLUE HAWAIIAN, C. 1920.
Anonymous, Hawaii, 80" x 99", cotton,
hand appliquéd and quilted.
Gift of The Binney Family, 1991.31.

The wives of nineteenth century missionaries
brought the tradition of quilting to Hawaii.
Beautiful arabesque designs on Hawaiian
quilts are thought to be an adaptation of the
Pennsylvania Dutch paper folding-and-cutting
technique of *scherenschnitte*, also probably
taught by the missionaries.

Legend says that the unique designs of
Hawaiian quilts were inspired after a woman
saw a shadow of a tree cast on a piece of
cloth drying in the sun. She thought the
pattern created was so beautiful that she
traced the shadow of the branches onto
fabric and made a quilt. The dense hand
quilting surrounding the designs is called
echo quilting, or *kuiki lau*.

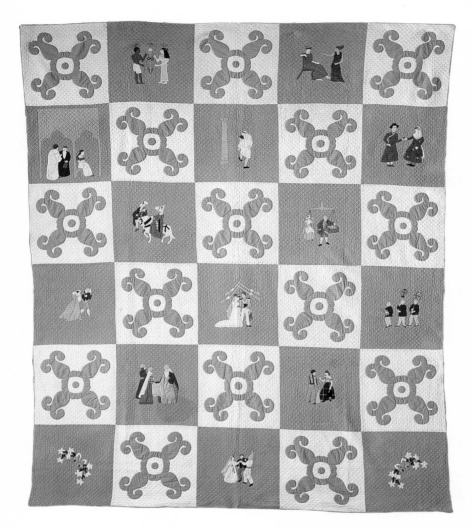

BRIDAL QUILT, 1952. Alice Shaner (Simpson), Story Book design by Marion Cheever Whiteside Newton, 86" x 105", cotton, hand appliquéd and quilted.

Gift of Alice Shaner-Simpson, 1998.07.

DETAIL FROM BRIDAL QUILT, MILITARY WEDDING BLOCK, 1952.

From 1940–1965 Marion Cheever Whiteside Newton operated a cottage industry under the patented Story Book label. She created over 50 appliqué quilt designs based on children's stories and popular themes.

Marion's quilts reflect an illustrator's approach to appliqué. For every Story Book quilt she designed, she researched costumes, characters, and details of the story or theme. As her business grew, Marion obtained requests for commissions: Mrs. John Hay Whitney and Mrs. Alfred G. Vanderbilt ordered horse-racing quilts for their husbands, and in the 1950s the Metropolitan Museum of Art in New York City commissioned an *Alice In Wonderland* quilt for their permanent collection.

Alice Shaner purchased the pattern for her quilt when she was sixteen years old for 25¢ from the *Ladies' Home Journal*. Since her parents worked in the covered button business, she made most of her quilt from scraps she found at home, although she did purchase the blue and white cotton and the pink for the faces. It took Alice three years to complete the appliqué, and another three years for the woman she hired to complete the hand quilting.

The success of the cottage industries was in large part responsible for the rise of quilt companies. In the 1930s, quilting became big business, and many of the companies that still cater to quilters were established. In 1933 Sears and Roebuck sponsored a quilt contest for the Century of Progress World's Fair in Chicago. The overwhelming response showed how popular quilting had become. Twenty-five thousand quilts were entered for a grand prize of $7,500 dollars. The prize-winning quilt was presented to First Lady Eleanor Roosevelt, but its whereabouts remain a mystery today.

Although the decline of quiltmaking in the 1940s is often attributed to the uncreative aspects of the pattern-based industry, the effects of World War II were equally responsible, if not more so. Women had less leisure time as they entered the workforce once reserved for men. Nationwide shortages of fabric and paper made quiltmaking a greater challenge.

---

[1] *Quilter's Journal* 3, no.4 (Winter 1980/1981), p.9 as quoted in Thos. K. Woodward & Blanche Greenstein, *Twentieth Century Quilts 1900-1950,* (E.P. Dutton: New York, 1988) , p. 1.

AMISH QUILTS

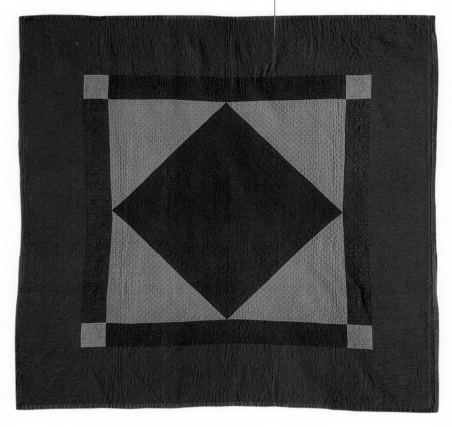

DIAMOND IN A SQUARE, C. 1910.
Unknown, embroidered "KK" with orange-red thread on one corner of the back of the quilt, Lancaster County, Pennsylvania, 73" x 74", wool, hand pieced and quilted.
Gift of The Binney Family, 1990.07.

Classic Amish quilts such as this suggest the landscape of farms; the simple planes of color represent the division of earth and sky. This quilt reflects the natural world: from far away, forms are simplified, but up close the image is complex and multifaceted.

The Amish came from Northern Europe to Lancaster, Pennsylvania in the 1730s seeking religious freedom. A second migration from 1816 to 1860 included the less-strict Mennonites, Moravians, and Lutherans, who settled in Ohio, Indiana, and Illinois. They trace their roots to the sixteenth century Swiss Anabaptists, a Protestant sect who believed in adult voluntary baptism. The established agrarian communities were small, homogenous, and isolated with distinct customs and religious beliefs. The Amish are known to us today for their pre-industrial lifestyle, unique dress, and beautiful quilts.

Although the Amish do not believe in religious art, they excel at traditional crafts such as quiltmaking. Amish quilts are simple, bright, and powerful. Solid, richly colored cottons and wools are set off by stark black fabric and intricate hand quilting. These quilts reflect the Amish belief in utilitarianism and their respect for a job well done.

Amish quilts hold a unique place in American art history. In 1971, the Whitney Museum of American Art exhibition, *Abstract Design in American Quilts*, from the collection of Jonathan Holstein and Gail van der Hoof, was the first major retrospective to distinguish American quilts as art. The simple forms, bold use of contrasting colors, and large planes of fabric of antique quilts were visually related to the modern American art movements of Abstract Expressionism, Minimal Art, and Color Field painting.

LOG CABIN VARIATION, 1890–1910.
Florence Bachstad,
Pennsylvania Mennonite, 71 ½" x 71 ½",
wool with black silk binding,
hand pieced and quilted.
Gift of The Binney Family, 1991.19.

This bold geometric pattern appeals to our late twentieth-century sensibilities. The contrasting colored wools create a dizzying effect, emphasized by the repeating design. The quilt gains further dimension by the maker's use of a folded, rather than a pressed, seam.

Some say that Amish and Mennonite quilts contain an intentional error and, indeed, one of the blocks in the border of this otherwise perfect quilt is reversed.

JACOB'S LADDER, 1925–1935.
Mrs. Jake J. Byler, New Wilmington,
Pennsylvania, 76 ½" x 84", cotton,
sateen, hand pieced and quilted.
Gift of The Binney Family, 1991.17.

Jacob's Ladder is more visually complex
than most traditional Amish quilts, probably
because the design was brought into the
community from the outside world.
Perhaps the religious nature of the pattern
made it appealing to Amish women.

In the Old Testament, God speaks
to Jacob in a vision and promises land to
his descendants. The blocks that go up
and down the quilt represent the ladder
from which angels ascend and descend
in Jacob's vision.

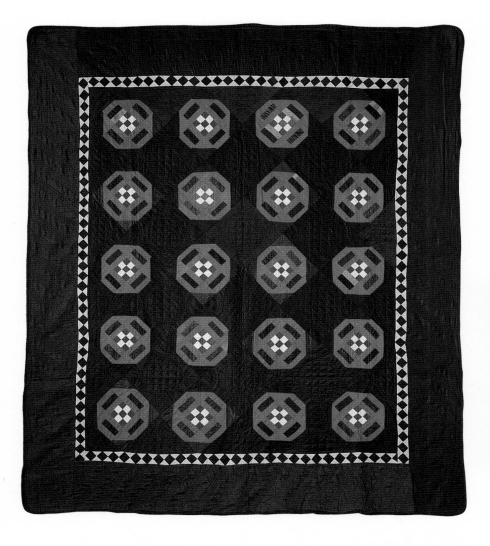

BURNAM SQUARE WITH NINE-PATCH CENTER, 1920–1940.
Ohio Amish, 71" x 84", cotton, sateen.
Gift of The Binney Family, 1991.18.

The Ohio Amish preferred piecework to quilting, and created many variations of the simple Nine-Patch pattern. These more intricate patterns are associated with the less strict lifestyles of Midwestern Amish communities, who allowed more trading among themselves and the outside world.

LOG CABIN BARN RAISING, 1875–1890.
Member of the Lentz family, Lebanon County, Pennsylvania, 76 ½" x 84",
wool challis, hand pieced and quilted.
Gift of The Binney Family, 1991.20.

OHIO STAR VARIATION, C. 1930.
Unknown, Ohio Amish, 68 ½" x 81",
cotton, sateen, hand pieced and quilted.
Gift of The Binney Family, 1989.03.

A distinctive feature of Amish quilts is the dark quilting thread; this Ohio Star Variation is quilted in tan and black. The quiltmaker may have used cinnamon or nutmeg to mark her quilt, indicated by brown stains at points along the quilting lines.

CONTEMPORARY QUILTS

The roots of quilting's revival in the late twentieth century began with turn-of-the-century European artists, such as Pablo Picasso, who broke away from traditional modes and materials in painting. European painters no longer looked to the masters of the Italian Renaissance for inspiration. Instead, they reached for the simple, powerful forms found in primitive art. While some artists borrowed from the art of Africa and Oceania, others, like those in the Blue Rider group that included Wassily Kandinsky, Paul Klee, and Gabriele Munter, were attracted to folk art and craft closer to home. They loved medieval icons and the art of German and Russian peasants—they seemed more direct and universal than traditional painting could be.

BLOODROOT, 1986.
Ruth McDowell, Winchester, Massachusetts, 114 ½" x 67",
satin, cotton, polyester, velvet, upholstery fabric, hand appliquéd, machine pieced, and hand quilted.
Gift of The New England Quilters Guild, 1986.03.

The natural world has inspired quiltmakers for centuries. Ruth McDowell continues this tradition in her interpretation of bloodroot flowers, which bloom in the spring in New England. *Bloodroot* is three-dimensional and double-sided—the flowers are stuffed and padded satin, and the stems are folded within two-sided, quilted leaves.

Meanwhile, in the United States, the Colonial Revival of the 1880s and the popularity of the British Arts and Crafts movement prompted an interest in finely made craft. Artists such as Louis Comfort Tiffany and John LaFarge approached the decorative arts with their full attention, artistry, and respect. In the next generation, Frank Lloyd Wright, the country's most famous architect, carried on this appreciation of fine craft.

The most influential group who applied the theories of fine art to the creation of industrial art were the artists associated with the Bauhaus School of Design, founded in Weimar, Germany, in 1919. Students approached art, architecture, and industrial design through studying the relationship between form and function. They applied the visual rules of modern art to everyday objects, made from everyday materials.

When the Nazis closed the school in 1925, many of the artist/teachers moved to the United States, where they continued their influential work. Following the German model, which included an emphasis on traditional crafts, the art world recognized Bauhaus-trained weavers such as Anni Albers. By the 1950s and 1960s, weaving was part of a formal curriculum at many art schools.

A revolution in attitudes toward textiles had arrived. Contemporary artists began to use cloth in their work: Claus Oldenberg's enormous soft sculptures, Christo's wrapped installations, and the very feminine textile creations of Eva Hess. Andy Warhol made indirect reference to quilt design in his silk-screened images of America's cultural icons, which rely on the repeated block format so recognizable in nineteenth-century quilts. Meanwhile, one of the most significant figures of modern art, Robert Rauschenberg, experimented with the quilt itself in his 1955 piece entitled *Bed*.

Studio-trained artists began to experiment with quiltmaking. Many of these artists were women who had sewn all their lives, now they joined both art and sewing. The first of these pieces were both beautiful and utilitarian, but many began to make quilts solely as fine art. The distinction between between art and craft blurred. Some artists created pieces with the physical characteristics of a utilitarian quilt. Many others worked outside the confines of traditional patterns, creating original designs and using experimental techniques to make quilts which hang like paintings.

As fiber artists expanded their focus, critics became aware of the artistic values of the previously overlooked American art form. Jonathan Holstein's 1971 exhibition exposed the New York art world to quilts as pure visual forms, and both collectors and museums took notice. Even before this pivotal exhibition, in 1965 the Newark Museum played up the similarity between painting and contemporary quilts in an exhibit entitled *Optical Quilts*. After the Whitney show, however, widespread recognition of quilts was truly underway.

New England was home to many of the first contemporary quilt artists and exhibitions. In 1975 both the Boston Center for the Arts and the Carpenter Center at Harvard University had exhibitions. The 1976 Bicentennial celebration irrevocably established the importance of quilts: like jazz music, they were honored as an unique American art form. It would still be a decade, however, before Michael Kile and Penny McMorris organized the 1986 traveling exhibition of contemporary quilts called *The Art Quilt,* which coined a term and solidified the movement.

The styles of contemporary quilts are as diverse as those of contemporary painters; there are quiltmakers who work with cubism, realism, surrealism, and formal abstraction. The new enthusiasm for quilts has reaffirmed three hundred years of women's quiltmaking and honored women as creators of one of America's most important art forms.

THREADS OF FRIENDSHIP, 1990. Members of The Cocheco Quilt Guild, Dover, New Hampshire, 72" x 72", cotton, hand pieced, appliquéd, and quilted. *Gift of The Cocheco Quilt Guild, 1995.02.*

This quilt, designed and made by members of the Cocheco Quilt Guild for the *Great American Quilt Festival III* in New York City, depicts a map of the states. Different regions are denoted with distinct fabrics and recognizable patterns. The patterns typify the areas: homespun material is used for the Northeast, a cowboy print for the Pacific Northwest, and wild and funky fabric for California.

LOOK THROUGH ANY WINDOW, 1990.
Natasha Kempers-Cullen, Topsham, Maine,
42 ½" x 64 ½", hand painted on cotton
with fiber reactive dyes, machine and hand
quilted. Embellished with beads,
buttons, slide mounts, and fabric pictures.
Gift of Natasha Kempers-Cullen, 1996.05.

Natasha uses paint and dye to re-create the
look of a pieced quilt, as in this whole-cloth
quilted painting. Kempers-Cullens also
embellishes the surfaces of her quilts with
a variety of beads and buttons. Here she
stitched rows of slide mounts to the surface
of the quilt; each one is backed with a
scrap of fabric. They all depict a person,
object, or scene as viewed through an
imaginary window.

Academia began to accept the quilt as well. In the early 1970s, feminist art historians called for a wider definition of fine art. They celebrated not only the minority of women artists working within the male art tradition, but also the vast number of anonymous women who worked in the female art tradition. Quilts, which are often a mature expression of a woman's artistic talent, were considered one of the most important of the feminine arts. Academics study quilts both as creative expression and as windows into the lives of everyday women.

The art quilt movement has grown tremendously in the past three decades. Quilters have experimented with and perfected a vast number of ways to enhance the surfaces of their quilts, including painting with dyes, photo transfer, and the inclusion of beads and found objects. Some concentrate on emotional expression, while others pursue new formal techniques.

ARCHIPELAGO, 1983.
Nancy Halpern, Natick, Massachusetts, 74 ½" x 96", cotton, cotton blends, hand pieced and hand quilted in an undulating pattern that echoes the movement of the ocean.
Gift of The New England Quilters Guild with funding provided by the Commonwealth of Massachusetts Council on the Arts and Humanities, 1983.01. Photo by David Caras.

The New England Quilters Guild commissioned this piece in 1982. It was unveiled at New England Images I, a quilt show organized by the New England Quilters Guild as a fundraiser for the opening of the New England Quilt Museum. *Archipelago* depicts the landscape off the coast of Maine; each house block represents an imaginary shelter where an artist friend lives and finds inspiration. This was the first quilt in the permanent collection, and the original house block from which Nancy developed her design is now the NEQM's logo.

CARE AND STORAGE OF TEXTILES

Compiled by Susan Wellnitz,
Associate Conservator,
American Textile History
Museum, Lowell

Textiles are made of organic materials: silk, wool, cotton, and linen. As the fiber is made into cloth, it is cleaned, spun, bleached, dyed, and woven, all of which contribute to the deterioration of fibers. Textiles are handled, stored, washed, and subjected to various temperature and humidity changes as they are passed from generation to generation. All of these factors contribute to the condition of quilts. We can't stop the aging process, but we can try to limit it.

CARE

LIGHT. While light is necessary for the pleasure of using and viewing textile objects, there is no "safe" amount of exposure to light. Light contributes to the accelerated aging of textiles and the fading of dyes. Under certain circumstances, light can cause chemical reactions that break down the fibers. All fabrics should be kept out of direct contact with the sun, and should be exhibited only briefly, alternating with longer periods of protective storage.

TEMPERATURE. The recommended environment for a textile is approximately 65° F and 50% relative humidity. Most attic and basement environments are unsafe for textiles; storing your quilts there can lead to damage from heat, mildew, mold, insects, and animals.

POLLUTION. Airborne contaminants like dust and smoke can accelerate fabric decay. Try to minimize your quilts' exposure to potential sources of deterioration: open windows and doors, heating and cooling vents, exhaust pipes, fireplaces, cooking areas, and uninsulated exterior walls.

VACUUMING. Vacuuming is a simple but effective way to remove some types of loose dirt from textiles. You should consider the condition and construction of a quilt before vacuuming it. Fabrics must be fairly strong and ornamentation must be securely attached to handle the suction from a vacuum cleaner. Any fabrics sensitive to abrasion, such as old silk, satins, velvets, and brocades, are not suitable for vacuuming. Also examine textiles with beads, sequins, or embroidery with special care; if the fabric is brittle and losing yarns and fiber, vacuuming will cause greater damage. The stitching that holds the embellishment in place may break, and fragile elements could come off completely. If the fabrics are shredding or powdering, or if your intuition tells you something doesn't look right, consult a professional conservator.

Work in a clean, well-lit area. Take a few moments to inspect the quilt for insects, mildew, mold, and other damage. Inspect your hanging system for signs of damage near the stitched areas. If you see evidence of a possible insect infestation, a mildew or mold problem, or obvious losses, seek the advice of a professional conservator before you do anything.

If vacuuming seems appropriate for your quilt, first make sure your vacuum has a variable suction control and a small brush attachment. Next, find a piece of fiberglass screening or nylon net approximately 20 inches square. Machine stitch white fabric tape around the perimeter of the screen to prevent it from snagging the fabric. This will protect the surface of your quilt as you clean.

Spread the quilt on a clean work surface, and place the screen or net over it. Reduce the suction on your vacuum so the fabric is not pulled upwards as you work. Move smoothly and systematically over the surface of the screen, raising and lowering the brush rather than rubbing it along the top of the screen. Use your free hand to hold everything in place under the brush. Lift the screen often to check your progress. Make sure the screen is not marring the surface of the quilt and that the suction is not loosening any decorative elements. Be especially careful near weak areas in the quilt and give special attention to seams and areas that have been protected from light and handling, where dust and insect debris often accumulate.

Place hand near area where vacuuming so the textile does not rise as the brush is raised.

Note: If you suspect the vacuum has collected insect debris or mildew, empty it immediately into a container outdoors.

DOCUMENTATION

Now that you've taken the time to protect your quilts from the damage of time, document them well. For easy access and minimal handling, place a photograph or detailed description of the piece in a clear sleeve attached to the outside of your storage system. Any records related to the quilt—oral history, stories of use and ownership, family trees, receipts, photographs, a history of repairs, historical significance, fabric scraps, and so on—will be an invaluable resource to anyone who wants to study the quilt in the future. Keep this information in a safe place.

STORAGE

Proper storage is a relatively inexpensive preventative conservation measure that every owner of a quilt can take. It protects quilts from migrating impurities, environmental soils, and damaging ultraviolet light. Ideally, quilts should be stored flat, in a temperature- and humidity-controlled dark space. Because these conditions are impractical or impossible for many of us, boxing and rolling are two safe alternatives for storing your quilts.

ROLLING YOUR QUILTS. Tubes for rolling should be sturdy, clean, and lightweight, with a minimum diameter of three inches. The larger the diameter, the less stress the fabrics will endure as you roll the quilt onto the tube. They should be at least six inches longer than the width of the piece in order to stick out three inches beyond the textile on either side. The extended tube gives a place to support or grip the rolled quilt without compressing the textile.

Tubes that are not acid-free require a barrier to prevent the quilt from being in direct contact with acidic properties in the tube. Mylar (a clear, uncoated polyester film) is a safe barrier. Wrap it around the tube and secure it with tape. You may want to wrap acid-free tissue or a washed piece of muslin around the tube a couple of times and leave at least a foot hanging free to become a header or starter for the quilt. Place the leading edge of the quilt on the header and roll evenly and smoothly; be careful to avoid wrinkling and rolling too tightly.

Certain textiles require a bit of special treatment. Fabrics with embellishments or irregular surfaces need an interlining of acid-free paper. Put the acid-free paper over the top of the quilt as you prepare it to go onto the tube, then roll the two together as one. Pile fabrics (such as corduroy or velvet) should be placed face-down on a clean surface and rolled in the direction of the pile. In general, lined fabrics should be rolled face-out. If repairs are sewn through the layers of your quilt or if there are severe wrinkles, distortions or weak areas, rolling may not be advisable. Seek the advice of a professional conservator if you are uncertain how to proceed.

Once you have rolled the quilt, wrap it in acid-free paper, washed muslin, or clean white sheeting. Whenever possible, the tubes should be supported from the ends, so the textile is suspended rather than resting on itself. Use cradles to lift each end, or roll bubble-wrap around the extended end of the tubes, but not around the quilt, until the quilt is raised above the storage shelf. If the fabrics are smooth and light, you may box the rolls or store them on shelves. Large tubes can be supported on dowels or pipes to avoid bowing in the middle.

Place quilt on a clean, well-lit work table. The first lengthwise fold is padded with a length of crumpled acid-free tissue.

The second lengthwise fold is padded.

The quilt is ready to be folded widthwise.

The quilt is now ready to go in the box.

BOXING YOUR QUILTS. Use boxes of archival quality, acid-free materials. They should be as long and wide as possible so you can put the quilt away with the fewest number of folds. Compare the measurements of the quilt and box before you start, and plan where to put the folds. To prevent creasing, pad the lengthwise and widthwise folds generously with crumpled, acid-free paper. Line the box with acid-free paper and place each folded quilt inside; don't overcrowd a single box with too many items.

The quilt is placed in the tissue-lined acid-free box.

DISPLAY

When you use or display your quilt, its location will determine how much wear it will suffer. Make sure the quilt is out of reach of pets or people who might handle it unnecessarily. Nearby furniture can make a useful barrier, but it shouldn't be so close that it rubs against the fabric, transferring dust and cleaning products. Vacuum the quilt periodically on both sides (see page 65 for guidelines) every six months unless the building is unusually dusty or heavily used. As you vacuum the quilt, take the opportunity to check for insect activity, soil, and signs of damage. Check the hanging system, too. If you used Velcro®, adjust it when necessary and press the sides together to re-establish firm contact. Quilts that lie folded on flat surfaces can be opened and folded along different lines. Try to avoid unnecessary folds and be sure to cushion the new folds with acid-free paper or white, well-washed sheeting.

Even under the most ideal conditions, quilts will age and be subject to deterioration. If you intend to donate your collection to a museum, to give heirloom gifts to your relatives, or to collect quilts for research and documentation, you can do so in a safe and informed manner. With proper care and a stable environment, quilts can last for generations.

SUPPLIERS

Archivart (Heller & Usdan)
P.O. Box 428
7 Caesar Place,
Moonachie, NJ 07074-1781
(201) 804-8986

Light Impressions
439 Monroe Avenue
Rochester, NY 14603
(800) 828-6216

University Products, Inc.
P.O. Box 101
517 Main Street
Holyoke, MA 01041
(800) 628-1912;
(800) 762-1165

Gaylord Brothers
P.O. Box 4901
Syracuse, NY 13221-4901
(800) 634-6307

GENERAL GUIDELINES

If you are new to quilting, please refer to one of the books about quilting listed under General Quilting References (page 94). Alex Anderson's Start Quilting (C&T, 1997) is a great place to start. The guidelines that follow are basic instructions.

SUPPLIES

- Sewing machine in good working order
  (We recommend starting any new project with a new needle.)
- Threads to match fabrics
- Scissors
- Iron and ironing board
- Pins
- Template plastic
  (for Butterflies and Log Cabin Variation 2)
- Freezer paper
  (for Log Cabin Variation 2)
- Seam ripper
- Rulers: a 6" x 24" and a 15" square see-through acrylic ruler
- Rotary cutter and mat
- Marking tools
- Quilting thread
- Embroidery thread
  (for Butterflies and Log Cabin Variation 2)

ROTARY CUTTING is used in most of the projects.

FABRIC Use 100% cotton. Although Log Cabin Variation 2 (page 84) was originally made with silks, it would be just as beautiful using cottons (and much less expensive!). We recommend pre-washing all of your fabric, especially if you are planning to make a quilt that will require laundering. Wash darks and lights separately by hand or using the soak cycle on your machine, then machine dry on the permanent press setting. Some quilters feel that prewashing fabrics that will be used in wallhangings or quilts that won't be laundered eliminates the chemicals used in the finishing processes, and makes the fabrics softer and therefore easier to hand quilt. Fabric requirements are based on a 42" width; many fabrics shrink when washed, and widths vary by manufacturer.

SEAM ALLOWANCES are 1/4". Please do a test seam before you begin sewing to check that your 1/4" is accurate.

PRESSING In general, press seams toward the darker fabric. Press lightly in an up-and-down motion. Avoid using a very hot iron or over-ironing, which can distort shapes and blocks.

BORDERS Measure your finished quilt top across the center both vertically and horizontally. Your final measurements may differ from the given measurements. Add 1/4" seam allowances to these measurements. Cut borders on the crosswise grain of the fabric. Diagonally piece the border strips together if necessary. Place pins at the centers of all four sides on the quilt top, then place pins at the centers of each border. Pin the side borders to the quilt top, matching the center pins. Sew and press. Repeat with the top and bottom borders. Trim as necessary. Borders of the Burgoyne Surrounded Variation quilt are mitered and instructions are given with the project.

BACKING Use 100% cotton for the backing; plan on making the backing a minimum of 2" larger than the quilt top on all sides. With the exception of the Variable Star wallhanging, the projects all require pieced backs. Pre-wash the fabric, and trim the selvages before you piece. To economize, you can piece the back from any leftover fabrics in your collection, or buy fabric and piece it according to the following diagrams.

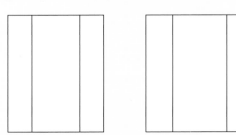
TWIN SIZE

FULL SIZE

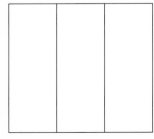
QUEEN OR KING SIZE

BATTING The type of batting to use is a personal decision; to achieve a more traditional, "antique" look you should consider using a very thin cotton batting, and then wash the quilt after you have finished quilting it. Some of the cotton battings can be bought by the yard; consult your local quilt shop. Cut batting approximately 2" larger on all sides than quilt top.

LAYERING Spread the backing wrong side up and tape the edges down. (If you are working on carpet you can use T-pins to secure the backing to the carpet.) Center the batting on top. Place the quilt top right side up on top of the batting and backing, making sure it's centered.

BASTING If you plan to machine quilt, pin baste the quilt layers together with safety pins placed every 3"–4" apart. Begin basting in the center and move toward the edges first in vertical, then horizontal, rows. If you plan to hand quilt, baste the layers together with thread using a long needle and light-colored thread. Using stitches approximately the length of the needle, begin in the center and move toward the edges.

QUILTING This is a personal decision. If you want to make a faithful reproduction study the photograph of the quilt you are making; in some of the projects quilting designs have been provided or discussed.

BINDING Trim excess batting and backing from the quilt. Cut binding strips 2^1/$_2$" wide, and piece the strips together with a diagonal seam to make one long, continuous binding strip. Press the seams open, then press the entire strip in half lengthwise with wrong sides together. With raw edges even, pin the binding to the edge of the quilt a few inches away from the corner, and leave the first few inches of the binding unattached. Start sewing, using a ^{1}/$_4$" seam allowance. Stop ^{1}/$_4$" away from the first corner and backstitch one stitch, and remove from the machine. Pivot the quilt counterclockwise. Fold the binding at a right angle so it extends straight above the quilt. Then bring the binding strip down even with the edge of the quilt. Begin sewing ^{1}/$_4$" away from the fold, backstitching after the first few stitches. Repeat in the same manner at all corners. Finish off the binding by overlapping the ends, and trim any leftover binding. Fold the binding over the raw edge to the back and blind stitch the binding to the back.

It's time to celebrate! You've created a beautiful heirloom.

Adding the Binding

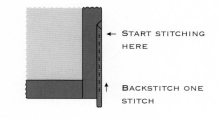

← START STITCHING HERE

↑ BACKSTITCH ONE STITCH

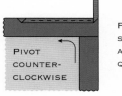

PIVOT COUNTER-CLOCKWISE

FOLD BINDING SO IT EXTENDS ABOVE THE QUILT

← START STITCHING HERE AND BACK-STITCH A FEW STITCHES

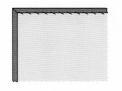

FOLD TO BACK AND BLIND STITCH

VARIABLE STAR

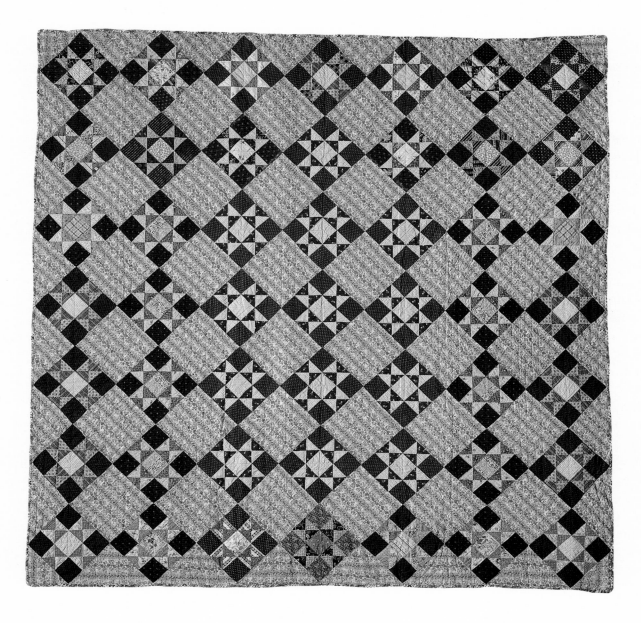

VARIABLE STAR, C. 1840.

Anonymous, 91" x 90", cotton, hand pieced and quilted.

Gift of Anne Gallo, 1990.21.

In the nineteenth century American quiltmakers made block style quilts in which small pieces of fabric were joined into blocks to form the top. The star was one of the most popular quilt patterns, and it appears in numerous variations throughout the history of quiltmaking.

Due to the rapid growth of the American textile industry a much wider variety of fabrics became available; the quiltmaker used a particularly rich array in this quilt. There are many indigo blue resist prints, fabrics boasting shaded floral designs accomplished by the use of picotage (pin-prick sized dots) outlines as well as rainbow-colored and delicate floral vine prints.

Fabric Tips: To make a reproduction of this quilt, use a variety of pinks, navys, browns, and beiges that would have been typical of the era. A neutral floral stripe would work well for the background fabric. This pattern would work just as well with your scrap collection or with bold contemporary colors.

FABRIC REQUIREMENTS

Instructions are provided for two different sizes: a wallhanging that measures approximately 39¼" square, and a quilt 90½" square that approximates the original.

WALLHANGING

Star Background:	½ yd. total
Star Body:	1 yd. total or scraps
Alternate Plain Blocks, and Side Setting and Corner Triangles:	1½ yds.
Backing:	1¼ yds.
Batting:	43" x 43"
Binding:	½ yd.

REPRODUCTION QUILT

Star Background:	2¾ yds. total
Star Body:	5½ yds. total
Alternate Plain Blocks, and Side Setting and Corner Triangles:	4 yds.
Backing:	7½ yds. (See diagram on page 68)
Batting:	94" x 94"
Binding:	⅔ yd.

Block Finished Size: 9"
Make nine blocks for the wallhanging
OR
forty-nine blocks for the reproduction quilt.

DETAIL OF VARIABLE STAR

Cutting

STAR BODY (for each star block)

Cut one $3^1/2$" square for the center. For the triangles around the center square, cut one $4^1/4$" square, then cut into quarter-square triangles. For star points, cut two $4^1/4$" squares, then cut into quarter-square triangles.

QUARTER-SQUARE TRIANGLES

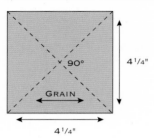

BACKGROUND (for each star block)

Cut four $3^1/2$" squares. Cut one $4^1/4$" square, then cut into quarter-square triangles.

ALTERNATE PLAIN BLOCKS

Cut four $9^1/2$" blocks for the wallhanging OR cut thirty-six $9^1/2$" blocks for the larger quilt.

SIDE SETTING TRIANGLES

Wallhanging:
Cut two 14" squares, then cut into quarter-square triangles.
Larger quilt:
Cut six 14" squares, then cut into quarter-square triangles.

CORNER TRIANGLES

(for both sizes)
Cut two $7^1/4$" squares, then cut into half-square triangles.

HALF-SQUARE TRIANGLES

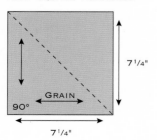

Block Assembly

Follow the diagrams below for the piecing sequence.

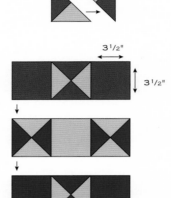

Quilt Assembly

Arrange your blocks following the setting diagram. Sew the blocks, corner, and side setting triangles into diagonal rows. Join the diagonal rows according to the diagram.

Quilting

Stitch $1/4$" inside seam line on all triangles; stitch a "cross" from corner to corner on the center 3" squares. Stitch vertical lines about 1" apart on alternate "plain" squares/blocks.

Please see page 69 in the General Guidelines for binding.

BUTTERFLIES

BUTTERFLIES, C. 1935.

Nina Shrock, Harvard County, Indiana, 86" x 93", cotton, hand and machine pieced and embroidered.

Gift of The Binney Family, 1991.12.

T he Great Depression of 1929 brought a national concern for thrift and frugality. The Work Relief Program of the Works Progress Administration was created to revitalize home crafts and community projects. The craft program, spearheaded by Eleanor Roosevelt, encouraged women in traditional American handicrafts. Scrapbag quilts, which are made from tiny "scraps" of fabric, were well suited to the American New Deal. In making such a quilt, a woman reinforced both her clever economy and her unique role as an American craftsperson. This Butterfly pattern was published by one of the most popular designers of the era, Laura Wheeler. The design reflects art deco styles in its curved arabesques and bold outlines, and is one of the favorite quilts in the NEQM's collection.

This pattern has been adapted from the original. It looks like an appliqué pattern but is actually pieced; the antennae of the butterflies are embroidered after the block is sewn. It's a perfect pattern for a scrap quilt, especially for the retro 1930s look with the reproduction fabrics that have become so popular in the last few years.

FABRIC REQUIREMENTS

Instructions are for an 84" x 93 1/2" (large full-size) quilt comprised of 72 blocks: 8 across x 9 down.

BUTTERFLIES (TEMPLATES A, B, C, D, E)

A	(Butterfly body)	1¼ yds. total scraps
B	(Wing curve)	1⅔ yds. total scraps
C	(Wing point)	1⅔ yds. total scraps
D	(Inner top of wing)	1¼ yds. total scraps
E	(Wing: Six pieces per block)	3 yds. total

BACKGROUND (TEMPLATES F, G, H, I), BORDERS, AND BINDING: 9 yds. total

Cut the borders on the lengthwise grain before you cut out the background templates.

BACKING	*(See diagram on page 68)*	6½ yds.
BATTING		88" x 97"

EMBROIDERY THREAD

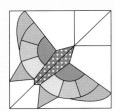

Block Finished Size: 9½"
Make seventy-two blocks.

Cutting

BORDERS

Cut on lengthwise grain of background fabric two 4½" x 85½" strips for side borders and two 4½" x 76½" strips for top and bottom borders.

BUTTERFLY TEMPLATES A, B, C, D, E *(For each block)*
Please see pages 91 and 92 for the template patterns.

A	(Butterfly body)	Cut one and one reverse
B	(Wing curve)	Cut one and one reverse
C	(Wing point)	Cut two
D	(Inner top of wing—solids were used in the original)	Cut two
E	(Wing)	Cut two from each of 3 different fabrics

BACKGROUND TEMPLATES F, G, H, I *(For each block)*

Cut one each of templates F, G, and H, then flip the template and cut a reverse. Template I doesn't have to be reversed, but you still need to cut two for each block. See suggested cutting diagram.

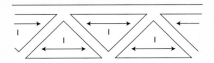

Block Assembly

Be sure to mark registration marks as indicated so that pieces can be lined up as you sew. Note the grain lines on your templates. **For each half-block** piece in the following order:

1. Sew the three E pieces together.

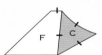

2. Sew B to G, lining up seam intersection and registration marks.

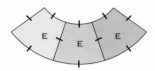

3. Sew C to F.

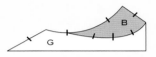

4. Sew the combined C/F unit to the B/G unit.

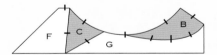

5. Sew the pieces created in Step 4 to the E unit that was created in Step 1. Make sure the registration lines meet. Do not sew beyond the seam intersection where C and F meet.

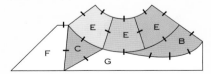

6. Sew D to the unit created in Step 5.

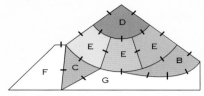

7. Sew H to I.

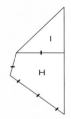

8. Sew the combined H/I unit to the combined unit created in Step 6; do not sew beyond the seam intersection where D and H meet.

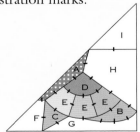

9. Sew A to the combined unit created in Step 8, matching registration marks.

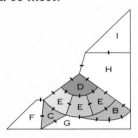

10. Sew both halves of the block together to complete the butterfly.

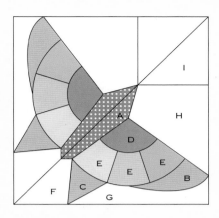

11. Embroider the antennae using a stem stitch. Refer to the cover for reference.

Quilt Assembly

1. Refer to the photo for block placement. Sew blocks into rows, then join rows together.

2. Add side borders first, then top and bottom borders.

Quilting

Quilt $1/4$" in from seam lines; placement of the leaf pattern is indicated on the template pattern pieces on page 91.

Binding

Please see page 69 in the General Guidelines for binding.

BURGOYNE SURROUNDED VARIATION

BURGOYNE SURROUNDED VARIATION, 1880-1900.

Anonymous, 79" x 96 ½", cotton, hand pieced and quilted.

Gift of the Binney Family, 1991.28.

This is a timeless pattern with a highly graphic, contemporary look. You can choose to follow the original indigo blue and white color scheme to make a faithful reproduction, or play with new color combinations to make your own statement.

The original border was appliquéd. The quilter placed diagonal strips that criss-crossed one another, with the center squares also appliquéd in the middle of the "block" formed by the strips. Our instructions utilize strip piecing and simple appliqué for ease of construction. You can also choose to complete the quilt with a simpler pieced border.

Fabric Tips: To make a reproduction, use a light-colored muslin or neutral tone-on-tone with a dark navy and white polka-dot print fabric for contrast. This would also be a great pattern to experiment with hand-dyed, batik, or marbleized fabrics for the darker pieces. Or you could sprinkle small photo transfers throughout the quilt in the 3" square pieces. You're limited only by your imagination.

FABRIC REQUIREMENTS

Instructions that follow are for a quilt 78" x 96".

DARK FABRIC	3$\frac{1}{2}$ yds.	*[includes inner border, outer border appliqué, and setting squares]*
LIGHT FABRIC	7$\frac{1}{2}$ yds.	*[includes sashing, outer border, and binding]*
BACKING	6$\frac{3}{4}$ yds.	*(See diagram on page 68.)*
BATTING	82" x 100"	

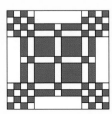

Block Finished Size: 15"
Make twelve blocks.

Cutting

A SET
Cut eight 3$\frac{1}{2}$"-wide strips (dark)
Cut four 1$\frac{1}{2}$"-wide (light)

B SET
Cut three 1$\frac{1}{2}$"-wide strips (dark)
Cut six 3$\frac{1}{2}$"-wide strips (light)

16-PATCH
Cut two 1$\frac{1}{2}$"-wide strips of both dark and light

FILLER STRIPS
Cut ten 2$\frac{1}{2}$"-wide strips from light fabric. Subcut these into forty-eight 2$\frac{1}{2}$" x 7$\frac{1}{2}$" strips.

SASHING STRIPS
Cut seventeen 3$\frac{1}{2}$" x 15$\frac{1}{2}$" strips from the light fabric

SETTING SQUARES
Cut six 3$\frac{1}{2}$" squares from the dark fabric

INNER BORDER
Cut two 2" x 51$\frac{1}{2}$" strips from the dark fabric for the top and bottom borders
Cut two 2" x 72$\frac{1}{2}$" strips from the dark fabric for the side borders

OUTER BORDER
Cut two 12$\frac{1}{2}$" x 85" strips from the light fabric for the top and bottom borders
Cut two 12$\frac{1}{2}$" x 104" strips from the light fabric for the side borders

STRIPS FOR OUTER BORDER APPLIQUÉ
Cut twenty-nine 2$\frac{1}{2}$"-wide strips from the dark fabric. Then subcut two of the strips into twenty-eight 2 $\frac{1}{2}$" squares.

Block Assembly
Finished Size: 15"

1. Begin the **Block Center** by sewing A Sets: Sew two $3^1/2$" dark strips to both sides of the $1^1/2$" light strip. Make four sets. Press seams toward the dark fabric. Subcut the sets into twenty-four $3^1/2$" units and forty-eight $1^1/2$" units.

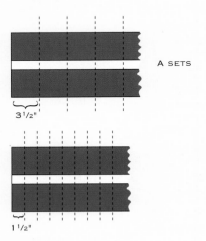

A SETS

$3^1/2$"

$1^1/2$"

B Sets are the same as A Sets, but with the dark and the lights reversed. Sew a $3^1/2$" light strip to each side of a $1^1/2$" dark strip. Make four sets. Press seams toward the dark fabric. Subcut the sets into sixty $1^1/2$" units.

2. To make twelve block centers, sew a $3^1/2$" A unit to each side of a $1^1/2$" B unit.

3. To make the **Side Units**, sew forty-eight pairs of $1^1/2$" A sets and $1^1/2$" B sets together. Sew each pair to a filler strip.

4. To make the **16-Patch**, sew the four strips together in the order shown. Subcut the sets into one-hundred and ninety-two $1^1/2$" units.

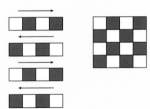

$1^1/2$"

5. Sew the units together as shown. Reverse every other row to form checkerboard.

6. Follow the piecing diagram below to assemble the **Burgoyne Surrounded** block. Sew two of the combined side-unit/fillers from Step 3 to opposite sides of a Block Center. Sew two 16-Patches to opposite sides of a pieced side-unit/filler; make two of these. You now have three "rows." Sew these together to complete the block.

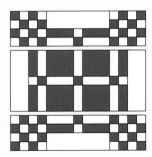

Quilt Assembly

1. Sew sashing strips to setting squares, then sew these units to the blocks following the construction diagram.

2. Sew the blocks into horizontal rows, then join these rows together.

3. Add the borders as follows.

Borders

Editor's note: *Because the quilt-maker made a lot of adjustments while making the borders in the original quilt, we have given approximated measurements. Allow yourself to be creative about placement of the strips and center squares. When it looks good, sew it!*

1. Sew the inner borders to the quilt top, starting and stopping $1/4$" from the edge. To miter the borders, place the quilt face down, smooth out one side of the border and mark a 45-degree angle starting at the inner corner. Reverse positions of the border, and again mark at 45 degrees. Line up the markings (with right sides together) and sew. Lay the quilt down flat. Make sure the corner is flat and even before trimming away the excess.

UNTRIMMED MITERED BORDER.

2. Sew the outer borders to the quilt top, starting and stopping 1/4" from the edge. Miter the border as in Step 1.

3. The diamond-shaped strips and inner squares are appliquéd on. The diamonds are formed by strips of fabric that are 1" wide when finished. Sew the strips together end to end to form one continuous strip. Then sew the long strip with wrong sides together, using a 1/4" seam. Press the seam open, center it in the back of the strip, and press the strip again.

4. The squares in the middle of the diamonds are 2" finished. Press under 1/4" on each edge of the 2 1/2" squares. For a crisp square, you can press using a 2" cardboard template as a guide.

5. Refer to the quilt diagram and photo of the quilt to see how the strips are placed on the border, and follow the diagram below. On the top, bottom, and corners the points of the diamonds are approximately 10 1/2" apart. On the sides, the points of the diamonds are approximately 10" apart. Place the corner diagonal strips first; mark approximately 21" from the outer corners of the border.

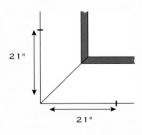

6. Pin the strip (centering on the marks), trim ends even with the border edge, and baste in place, leaving an opening at the mitered seam for the next step. Do all four corners before continuing.

7. Pin a strip centered on top of the mitered seam, tuck the end under the first strip, trim the outer end even with the border edge, and baste in place. Do all four corners before continuing.

8. Beginning at the edge of the first strip, using chalk and a ruler, mark the top and bottom borders approximately 10 1/2" apart.

9. Mark the side borders approximately 10" apart.

START MEASURING HERE

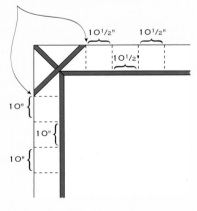

10. Begin pinning the strip in place, folding it over itself at an angle to create a mitered point. Align the mitered points with the chalk marks. (See diagram below) Pin the strip all the way around; then make adjustments as needed until the diamonds appear balanced and even. [**Note:** They will not be perfect; this is where your personal creativity comes into play.]

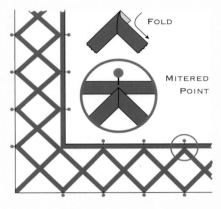

11. Baste the strips in place and appliqué to the border.

12. After the strips are sewn, mark the locations of the center squares by marking an "X" in the center of each diamond, using the corners of the diamonds as guides. Pin, baste, and sew the squares.

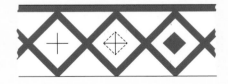

Quilting

Follow the diagram for the overall grid quilting and for placement of the quilted flowers if you choose to reproduce the original quilting design.

Binding

Please see page 69 in the General Guidelines for binding.

LOG CABIN VARIATION 1

LOG CABIN VARIATION, C. 1930.

Anonymous, 70" x 70", cotton, sateen, hand pieced and quilted.

Gift of Bruce and Nancy Berman, 1998.01.

T his variation on the Log Cabin pattern has strength in its graphic, contemporary appeal. The quiltmaker's use of color is striking, and the overall visual aesthetic is very modern. The origins of this quilt are unknown, but its bold design and use of cotton and sateens could indicate an Ohio Amish influence.

This quilt is fun to make because you can be so spontaneous with color. You can forego the typical assembly-line sewing order and make each block different. Also consider other colorways; traditional Amish colors would be beautiful, as would pastels or neutrals.

Fabric Tips: This is a great candidate for polished cottons, hand-dyed fabrics, or any other solids you choose to use.

FABRIC REQUIREMENTS

The following instructions are for a somewhat smaller version of the original; this quilt measures 60" square.

BLOCKS	1/4 yd. each of a minimum of six different colors 1/4 yd. should yield six 1 1/2"-wide strips. Strips of one color can be cut from the leftover border or backing fabric.
BORDER	1 5/8 yds. for unpieced borders OR 3/4 yd. for pieced borders
BACKING	3 1/2 yds. (leftover fabric can be used for block centers or strips)
BATTING	64" x 64"
BINDING	1/2 yd.

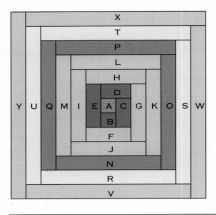

Block Finished Size: 13"
Make sixteen blocks.

Cutting

BORDERS

If you choose to use unpieced borders, cut the border strips first. Cut two 4 1/2" x 52" strips for sides and two 4 1/2" x 60 1/2" strips for top and bottom. You can use the leftover fabric to cut strips for the blocks.

STRIPS

Cut two strips 1 1/2"-wide by width of fabric from each of your fabrics. You start with a long strip and trim as you complete each round of sewing, following the construction diagrams. You will need to cut more strips after you have sewn a few blocks, but two cut strips will get you started sewing—the fun part!

Block Assembly

The blocks are constructed in a typical log cabin fashion, but are not divided into light/dark halves. Instead, same-color strips are added in rounds around the center square. The center and first strip are both squares; the rest of the logs are rectangles.

1. Cut a 1¹/₂" square from each color strip chosen for center square A and first square B.

2. Sew the center square A and the first square B (color 2) with right sides together. Press toward square B.

3. Using a long strip of color 2 for C, place it right sides together on the AB unit. Sew, making sure B is on the bottom. Press open and trim C even with the top and bottom of the AB unit.

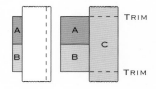

4. Continuing with the same color strip (2), place D right sides together on top of the ABC unit. Sew, press, and trim.

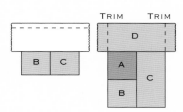

5. Using color 2 for the last time in this round, place the E strip right sides together with the ABCD unit as shown. Sew, press, and trim.

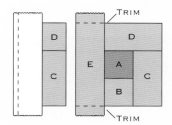

6. Change to your next color, and add strips F, G, H, and I in the same fashion, working your way around the block. Press and trim as you go. Refer to the block diagram as you add each strip. After you complete each round check the block with a square acrylic ruler to make sure it is square.

7. Change to your next color, and add strips J, K, L, and M. Check the squareness of the block.

8. Change to the next color, and add strips N, O, P, Q. Check the squareness of the block.

9. Change to the next color, and add strips R, S, T, U. Check the squareness of the block.

10. Change to the next color, and add the final strips V, W, X, and Y. Your completed block should be 13¹/₂" square.

11. Make 15 other blocks in the same way, changing the colors within each block.

Quilt Assembly

Lay out your blocks on a design wall or a large piece of batting tacked to a wall. When you are pleased with the block arrangement you can begin sewing the blocks into rows.

Take care to keep the blocks in the desired order as you remove them from the arrangement; it helps to pin a scrap of paper to each block with a notation of its order in the quilt. Sew the blocks together in horizontal rows. Press the seams of each row in alternate directions; that way, when you sew the rows together the seams will butt together and lay flat when sewn.

Please see page 68-69 in the General Guidelines for adding borders and binding.

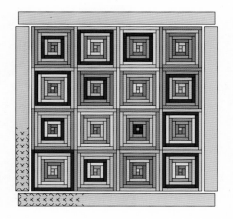

Quilting

The original quiltmaker quilted just outside all of the seam lines within each block, and finished her quilting with rows of diagonal quilting on the outside borders. A simple all-over grid of diagonal crosshatching would also work well.

LOG CABIN VARIATION 2

SILK LOG CABIN, 1880-1900.

Anonymous, 61" x 61", silk, satin, brocade, hand pieced and quilted, and embroidered.

Gift of the Binney Family, 1991.21.

og Cabin variations were the popular patterns to execute in silks, satins, and velvets. The pieced fans in the four corners of this quilt contain silk embroidery. Fans are a common reference to the popularity of Japanese decorative arts during the Victorian era.

Instructions are included for the four pieced fan blocks in the corners of the border; you could also use a simpler, single-fabric corner, or use solid black borders.

Fabric Tips: Break the bank and use silks as in the original? The more practical way to go would be to look for fabrics with a sheen: polished cotton, sateens, or the 100% solid cottons with gold or silver flecks that are currently available. For the blue fabric you could use a subtle tone-on-tone.

FABRIC REQUIREMENTS

The following instructions are for a quilt that measures approximately 75" square.

BLOCKS	1 yd.	yellow
	$3^{3}/_{4}$ yds.	blue
	$6^{1}/_{4}$ yds.	black (includes unpieced borders and binding)
BACKING	$4^{1}/_{2}$ yds.	
BATTING	79" x 79"	

Block Finished Size: $7^{1}/_{2}$"

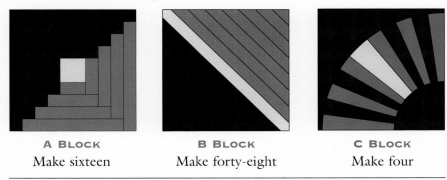

| **A BLOCK** | **B BLOCK** | **C BLOCK** |
| Make sixteen | Make forty-eight | Make four |

Cutting

A BLOCKS

Cut one 2"-wide strip of yellow
Cut fifteen $1^{1}/_{4}$"-wide strips of blue
Cut seventeen $1^{1}/_{4}$"-wide strips of black
Note: Because you add the strips in a progressive "from-the-center-out" style, you start with 42" strips, and trim each strip as you sew.

B BLOCKS

Cut sixteen $1^{1}/_{4}$"-wide strips of yellow
Cut sixty-three $1^{1}/_{4}$"-wide strips of blue
Cut sixty-three $1^{1}/_{4}$"-wide strips of black
Note: These will also be trimmed as you sew.

C BLOCKS

Please see page 92 for the template patterns for this block.
Cut four templates A and B and four B Reverse from black
Cut four template C from yellow
Cut twenty-four template D from blue
Cut sixteen template D from black

BORDERS

If you are making C blocks for the corners cut four 8" x $60^{1}/_{2}$" black strips for the borders. If you are *not* making C blocks and will be using solid borders, cut two 8" x $60^{1}/_{2}$" strips for the side borders and two 8"x $75^{1}/_{2}$" strips for the top and bottom borders. Please see page 68 in the General Guidelines for adding borders.

A Block Assembly

1. Make sixteen A Blocks, a typical Log Cabin block with a yellow 1 1/2" (finished) center square, and black and blue 3/4" (finished) logs. Follow the piecing sequence shown in the block diagram. The blocks are constructed in much the same way as the Log Cabin blocks in Variation 1 as described on page 82, except the second piece in this block is a rectangle, not a square.

With right sides together sew a blue strip to the yellow strip. Press the seam toward the blue strip. Subcut this into 2" units.

2. Sew the blue strip onto the right side of the first unit. Press and trim even with the raw edge of the first unit. You will use what remains of the blue strip in Step 4 for succeeding blue rounds.

3. Change to a black strip and sew it right sides together to the top of the unit created in steps 1 and 2. Press toward the black strip and trim. Sew the remaining black strip to the left of the sewn unit, press toward the black and trim. Measure the partial block you have sewn; it should be 3 1/2" square.

4. Continue sewing, pressing, and trimming until the block is finished (four rounds of each color). The completed block should measure 8" square.

B Block Assembly

Make forty-eight B Blocks, which resemble a Roman Stripe block. This block is made with a foundation such as freezer or tracing paper.

1. Cut forty-eight pieces of paper 8" square. Mark a line on the diagonal as shown, and then mark lines 5/8" from either side of the diagonal. These act as guidelines for placement of the 1 1/4" yellow strip.

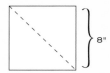

2. Place the yellow strip right side up between your guidelines and pin in place along the center diagonal.

Place the first blue strip right sides together on top of the yellow. Sew the strips together on the left diagonal using the raw edges of the strips as a guideline, a 1/4" seam allowance, and a very short stitch length (approximately 16-18 stitches per inch). Press the seam using a medium-hot iron to lock the stitches; flip open, and press again. Trim even with the outside edge of the paper.

3. Place a black strip on top of the yellow, right sides together, and sew on the right diagonal. Press, flip open, press again, and trim.

Now that the center strip is anchored on each side, you can remove the pins from the yellow strip. Continue adding black strips to one side, blue strips to the other, pressing and trimming the strips as you go, until you've added six strips on each side. The last strip will be trimmed so it looks like a small triangle.

4. Repeat this process for a total of forty-eight blocks. Before you can sew the blocks together, you will need to remove the freezer paper. This is not the fun part, so turn on your favorite radio station or TV program (HGTV's "Simply Quilts" would be inspiring), or rent a movie like "How to Make an American Quilt." Starting at one corner, fold the paper toward the first line of stitching, then gently tear the paper down the seam line. Loosen the paper under the next seam, fold, and tear. Repeat diagonally across the block. It will take a while, but the accuracy of the blocks is worth the extra time it takes to remove the paper.

C Block Assembly

Note: After tracing pattern pieces onto template plastic with an ultra-fine permanent pen, cut templates apart just *inside* the lines. Mark each tempalte with its grain line, block name, template letter, and any registration and intersection lines.

1. Make four C Blocks for the corners of the borders. Lay out the fan pieces in the order shown in the diagram.

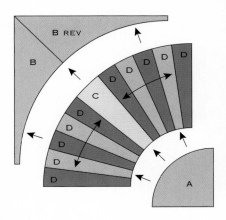

Sew a blue D to each side of a yellow C; then sew a black D to each side of the blue D-yellow C-blue D unit. Complete the fan alternating blue and black Ds.

2. Sew B to B reverse. Sew this unit to the top of the fan section.

3. To complete the block, sew A to the base of the fan section.

Quilt Assembly

1. Lay out the blocks as in the diagram. Sew the blocks together first in horizontal rows, then join the horizontal rows together.

2. If you have made the C Blocks for the corners, first add the side borders to the quilt top using a $1/4$" seam allowance. Sew the C blocks to each end of both the top and bottom borders following the diagram, and sew these to the top and bottom of the quilt top.

3. Embroider the edges of the fan with a feather or fly stitch in yellow embroidery thread as shown in the original quilt.

Quilting

The quiltmaker chose a cable design for the borders. Stitching in the ditch or an all-over grid would well work for the interior of the quilt.

Binding

Please see page 69 in the General Guidelines for adding binding.

Anonymous, Boston, Massachusetts, 59 ½" x 81 ½", cottons; multicolored prints
and solids on cream ground, bound quilt top, appliquéd and pieced.

Gift of Shirley Taft Gibbons, 1988.05.

The maker of this quilt used a variety of home decorator and eye-catching nineteenth century prints to make her cotton crazy quilt. Some of the most interesting include: blue and white monochromes, chinoiserie prints (fabrics with oriental designs) from the 1840s, "cheater" cloth, (printed fabrics such as the cat's face, the bird and the horseshoe); and furnishing fabrics (badminton players, lambs, and large-scale flowers). The piece is whimsical with the badminton players placed alongside large-scale flowers and animals. The title Boston Pavement refers to the cobblestone streets of Boston. Indeed, other quilts in public collections with a similar pattern are called The Streets of Boston.

The original quilt is five blocks wide by seven blocks long. The scraps are cut in irregular shapes and appliquéd onto the foundation.

In making a reproduction of this type of quilt, you can choose to use muslin or tone-on-tone prints as the foundation fabric. Scraps of any type of fabric can be used: novelty prints; vintage fabrics such as tea towels, flour sacks, handkerchiefs, bed linens, vintage clothing, ribbon, scraps from your children's or grandchildren's clothing; toile de jouy; any type of ethnic fabrics; parts of "cheater panels"; the possibilities are limitless.

FABRIC REQUIREMENTS

Instructions that follow are for a quilt approximately 52" x 82".

BLOCKS	4½ yds.	For foundation fabric
		Variety of scraps for appliqué
BINDING	1 yd.	

Block Finished Size: 11½"
Make thirty-five blocks.

Cutting

1. Cut twelve 13"-wide strips of foundation fabric. Then cut strips into thirty-five 13" squares. Blocks will be squared after all the shapes are appliquéd onto the foundation.

2. Cut appliqué shapes to suit the individual fabrics and blocks, one at a time.

Block Assembly

1. Fold and finger press foundation squares in half in both directions in order to find the center of the block.

2. Arrange the appliqué shapes on the foundation squares to fit within an 11" square. This allows for 1" beyond the appliqué shapes on each side. Allow for ¼" to ½" between shapes (after they are appliquéd) as in the original quilt top.

Tip: Make an 11" square template from tracing paper. Fold in half in both directions to find the center. Use this to assist in fitting appliqué shapes within an 11" square.

3. Pin or thread baste the shapes in place, then appliqué in your favorite manner.

4. Arrange the blocks in a straight set of five across and seven down to determine which will be the corner, side, and inside blocks. Label each block's position.

5. The four corner blocks (Block A) are squared/trimmed to 12¹/₂" square, allowing for 1" beyond the appliqué shapes on the two outside edges, and ¹/₂" on the two inside edges.

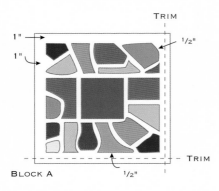

BLOCK A

TRIM FOUR BLOCKS FOR CORNERS: 1" ON TWO SIDES BEYOND APPLIQUÉ SHAPES, AND LEAVE ¹/₂" ON TWO SIDES.

6. Trim the sixteen side blocks (Block B) to be 12¹/₂" x 12", allowing for 1" beyond the appliqué shapes on the one outside edge, and ¹/₂" on the three inside edges.

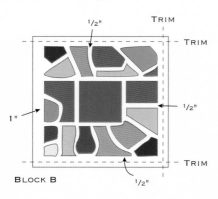

BLOCK B

TRIM SIXTEEN BLOCKS FOR SIDES: 1" ON ONE SIDE BEYOND APPLIQUÉ SHAPES, AND LEAVE ¹/₂" ON THREE SIDES.

7. Trim the fifteen inside blocks (Block C) to 12" square, allowing for ¹/₂" beyond the appliqué shapes on all four edges.

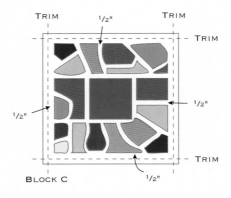

BLOCK C

TRIM FIFTEEN BLOCKS FOR INTERIOR: 12" SQUARE, LEAVING ¹/₂" BEYOND APPLIQUÉ SHAPES ON FOUR SIDES.

8. Lay out the blocks as in the diagram and sew them together into rows, then join the rows together.

A	B	B	B	A
B	C	C	C	B
B	C	C	C	B
B	C	C	C	B
B	C	C	C	B
B	C	C	C	B
A	B	B	B	A

9. Bind the quilt top. Please see page 69 in General Guidelines.

Note: No batting or backing was used to make the original quilt. As noted in the photo caption, this quilt was a bound top. Batting and backing could be added if preferred.

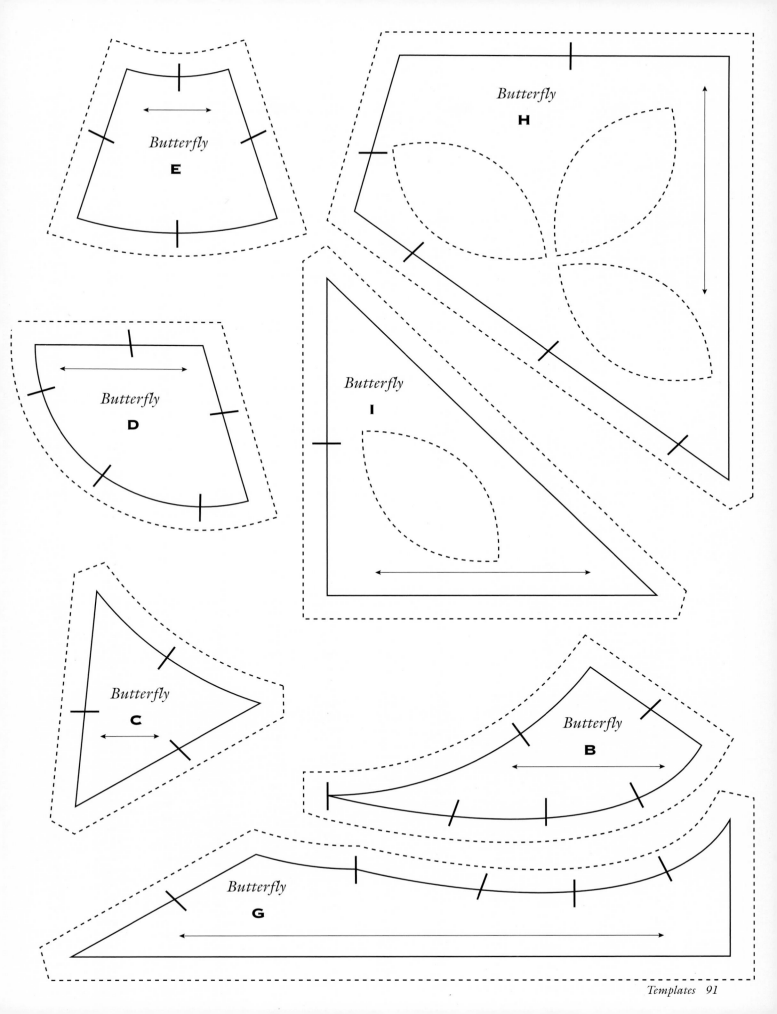

Butterfly
E

Butterfly
H

Butterfly
D

Butterfly
I

Butterfly
C

Butterfly
B

Butterfly
G

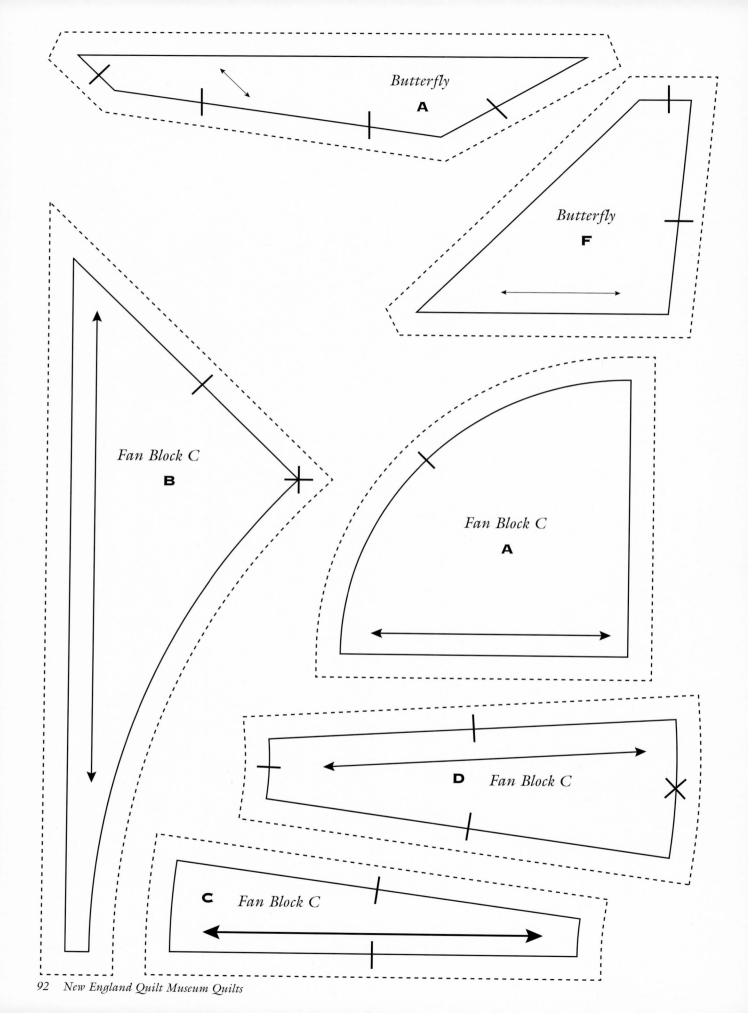

Butterfly
A

Butterfly
F

Fan Block C
B

Fan Block C
A

D Fan Block C

C Fan Block C

Adamson, Jeremy. *Calico and Chintz: Antique Quilts from the Collection of Patricia S. Smith*. Washington: Renwick Gallery of the National Museum of American Art, Smithsonian Institution, 1997

Ames, Kenneth. *Death in the Dining Room and other Tales of Victorian Culture*. Philadelphia: Temple University Press, 1992.

Anonymous, *"New England Factory Life,"* Harper's Weekly vol. 12 (July 25, 1868); 471.

Anonymous, *"Gold Watches,"* The Lowell Offering Series II vol 2, (1842); 377-379.

Axelrod, Alan, ed. *The Colonial Revival in America*. New York: Norton for The Henry Francis du Pont Winterthur Museum, 1985.

Bacon, Lenice. *American Patchwork Quilts*. New York: William Morrow & Co., 1973.

Bassett, Lynne Z. and Larkin, Jack. *Northern Comfort: New England's Early Quilts, 1780-1850*. Nashville, TN: Rutledge Hill Press for Old Sturbridge Village, 1998.

Baxandall, Rosalyn; Gordon, Linda; and Reverby, Susan, eds., *America's Working Women*. New York: Vintage Books, 1976.

Bean, Caroline, *"Dignity of Labor,"* The Lowell Offering Series II vol. 2, (1842); 192.

Blewett, Mary H., ed. *Caught Between Two Worlds: The Diary of a Lowell Mill Girl, Susan Brown of Epsom, New Hampshire*. Lowell, MA: Lowell Museum, 1984.

Bonfield, Lynn A., *"The Production of Cloth, Clothing, and Quilts in 19th Century New England Homes,"* Uncoverings 1981, vol. 2 edited by Sally Garouette, Mill Valley, CA: American Quilt Study Group, 1982; 77-96.

Bonfield, Lynn A., *"Diaries of New England Quilters Before 1860,"* Uncoverings 1988, vol. 9 edited by Sally Garouette, Mill Valley, CA: American Quilt Study Group, 1989; 171-197.

Brown, Dee Alexander. *The Year of the Century: 1876*. New York: Charles Scribner's Sons, 1966.

Burns, Sarah. *Pastoral Inventions: rural life in nineteenth-century American life and culture*. Philadelphia: Temple University Press, 1989.

Cott, Nancy F. *The Bonds of Womanhood: "Woman's Sphere" in New England, 1780-1835*. New Haven, CT: Yale University Press, 1977.

Cott, Nancy F., ed. *Root of Bitterness: Documents of the Social History of American Women*. New York: E.P. Dutton and Co, Inc., 1972.

Cozart, Dorothy. *"When the Smoke Cleared,"* The Quilt Digest vol. 5 (San Francisco: The Quilt Digest Press, 1987); 50-57.

Dublin, Thomas. *Lowell: The Story of an Industrial City: a guide to Lowell National Historical Park and Lowell Heritage State Park*. Lowell, MA: National Park Service, 1992.

Dublin, Thomas. *Women at Work: The Transformation of Work and Community in Lowell Massachusetts, 1826-1860*. New York: Columbia University Press, 1979.

Dunivent, Beverly. *"1930's Revisited."* Quilting Today. vol. 23 (Feb/March 1991); 10, 13, 27.

Dunivent, Beverly and Copeland, Anne. *"Kit Quilts in Perspective,"* Uncoverings 1993, vol. 15 edited by Sally Garouette, Mill Valley, CA: American Quilt Study Group, 1994; 141-167.

Dunivent, Beverly and Copeland, Anne. *"Quilt Kits; More Than Just Quilt-By-Numbers,"* American Quilter. vol. 20, no. 4 (Winter 1994); 22-24.

Eisler, Benita, ed. *The Lowell Offering: Writings by New England Mill Women 1840-1845*. Philadelphia: J.P. Lippincott, 1977.

Eno, Arthur L., Jr., ed. *Cotton Was King*. New Hampshire Publishing Company: Lowell Historical Society, 1976.

Fagan Affleck, Diane L. *Just New From the Mills: Printed Cottons in America*. North Andover, MA: Museum of American Textile History, 1987.

Federico, Jean Taylor. *"White Work Classification System,"* Quilter's Journal vol 3. no. 1, 1980; 19-20.

Foner, Philip S. *Women and the American Labor Movement: From Colonial Times to the Eve of World War I*. New York: The Free Press, 1979.

Foner, Philip S. *The Factory Girls*. Urbana, IL: University of Illinois Press, 1977.

Fry, Gladys-Marie. *Stitched from the Soul: Slave Quilts from the Ante-Bellum South*. New York: Dutton Studio Books in association with the Museum of American Folk Art, 1990.

Frye, L. Thomas, ed. *American Quilts: A Handmade Legacy*. Exh. cat. The Oakland Museum; 1981.

Garouette, Sally. *"Early Colonial Quilts in a Bedding Context,"* Uncoverings 1980, vol. 1 edited by Sally Garouette, Mill Valley, CA: American Quilt Study Group, 1981; 18-27.

Grier, Katherine C. *Culture and Comfort: People, Parlors, and Upholstery, 1850-1930*. Rochester, NY: The Strong Museum, 1988.

Gunn, Virginia. *"Crazy Quilts and Outline Quilts: Popular Responses to the Decorative Art/Art Needlework Movement, 1876-1893,"* Uncoverings 1984, vol. 5 edited by Sally Garouette, Mill Valley, CA: American Quilt Study Group, 1985; 131-152.

Gunn, Virginia. *"Victorian Silk Template Patchwork in American Periodicals, 1850-1875,"* Uncoverings 1983, vol. 4 edited by Sally Garouette, Mill Valley, CA: American Quilt Study Group; 9-25.

Gutman, Herbert G., ed. *Who Built America? Working People and the Nation's Economy, Politics, Culture, and Society*. (2 vols.) New York: Pantheon Books, 1989.

Hefford, Wendy. *Design for Printed Textiles in England from 1750 to 1850*. New York: Canopy Books; London: Victoria and Albert Museum, 1992.

Homage to Amanda: Two Hundred Years of American Quilts from the Collection of Edwin Binney, 3rd & Gail Binney-Winslow. Exh. cat San Francisco: R.K. Press, 1984.

Horton, Laurel. *"Glorified Patchwork: South Carolina Crazy Quilts,"* South Carolina: McKissick Museum, the University of South Carolina, 1989.

Hughes, Robert. *American Visions: The Epic History of Art in America*. New York: Alfred A. Knopf, 1997.

Kulik, Gary; Park, Roger; and Penn, Theodore Z. *The New England Mill Village, 1790-1860*. Cambridge, MA: MIT Press, 1982.

Larcom, Lucy. *A New England Girlhood Outlined from Memory*. Williamstown, VA: Corner House, 1889.

Lichten, Frances. *Decorative Art of Victoria's Era*. New York: Charles Scribner's Sons, 1950.

Lipsett, Linda Otto, *Remember Me: Women and Their Friendship Quilts*. San Francisco: The Quilt Digest Press, 1985.

Maciver, Percival. *The Chintz Book*. London: William Heinemann, Ltd., 1923.

McMorris, Penny. *Crazy Quilts*. New York: E.P. Dutton, 1984.

McMorris, Penny. "Victorian Style: *Vintage Photographs on an American Home,*" *The Quilt Digest vol. 2* San Francisco: 1984; 26-33.

McMorris, Penny and Kile, Michael. *The Art Quilt.* San Francisco: The Quilt Digest Press, 1986.

Meller, Susan and Elffers, Joost. *Textile Designs.* New York: Harry N. Abrams, 1991.

Montgomery, Florence M. *Printed Textiles: English and American cottons and linens 1700-1850.* New York: Viking Press, 1970.

Norkunas, Martha K. *"Women, Work and Ethnic Identity: Personal Narratives and the Ethnic Enclave in the Textile City of Lowell, MA."* The Journal of Ethnic Studies 15:3 (1987) 27-48.

Orlofsky, Myron and Patsy Orlofsky. *Quilts in America.* New York: McGraw Hill, 1974.

Pilgrim, Paul D. and Roy, Gerald E. *Victorian Quilts 1875-1900: They Aren't All Crazy.* Exh cat. Paducah, KY: American Quilters' Society: 1984.

Preston, Jo Anne. *"Millgirl Narratives: Representations of Class and Gender in Nineteenth-Century Lowell,"* Life Stories, 1987; 21-29.

Ramsey, Bets. *"Art and Quilts: 1950-1970,"* Uncoverings 14 (1993), edited by Sally Garouette, Mill Valley, CA: American Quilt Study Group; 9-40.

Rhoades, William Bertholet. *The Colonial Revival.* New York: Garland, 1977.

Roth, Rodris. *"The Colonial Revival and Centennial Furniture." Art Quarterly* 27:1 (1964); 57-81.

Rybicki, Verena M. *"On the Trail of the Lowell Crazy Quilt." Traditional Quilter* (June 1991); 45-47.

Safford, Carleton L., and Bishop, Robert. *America's Quilts and Coverlets.* New York: E.P. Dutton, 1972.

Schoeser, Mary and Rufey, Celia. *English and American Textiles: from 1790 to the present.* New York: Thames and Hudson, 1989.

Selden, Bernice. *The Mill Girls: Lucy Larcom, Harriet Hanson Robinson, Sarah G. Bagley.* New York: Antheneum, 1983.

Shaw, Robert. *Quilts: A Living Tradition.* New York: Hugh Lauter Levin Assoc., 1995.

Shaw, Robert. *The Art Quilt.* New York: Hugh Lauter Levin Assoc., 1997.

Sullivan, Kathleen, *Gatherings: America's Quilt Heritage.* Exh. cat. Paducah, KY: American Quilter's Society, 1995.

Swan, Susan Burrows. *Plain and Fancy: American Women and Their Needlework, 1700-1850.* New York: Holt, Rinehart and Winston, 1977.

Robinson, Harriet Hobson. *Loom and Spindle; or, Life Among the Early Mill Girls.* New York: T.Y. Crowell, 1898.

Townsend, Louise O., *"The Great American Quilt Classics: New York Beauty." Quilter's Newsletter Magazine* 131 (April 1991); 10-11.

Waldvogel, Merikay. *Soft Covers for Hard Times: Quiltmaking and the Great Depression.* Nashville: Rutledge Hill Press, 1990.

Waldvogel, Merikay and Brackman, Barbara. *Patchwork Souvenirs of the 1933 World's Fair.* Nashville, TN: Rutledge Hill Press, 1993.

Weible, Robert, ed. *The Continuing Revolution: A History of Lowell, MA.* Lowell, MA: Lowell Historical Society, 1991.

Wheeler, Candace. *Principles of Home Decoration.* New York: Doubleday Press, 1908.

Woodward, Thomas K. and Greenstein, Blanche. *Twentieth Century Quilts 1900-1950.* New York: E.P. Dutton, 1988.

General Quilting References

Anderson, Alex. *Start Quilting.* Lafayette, CA: C&T Publishing, 1997.

Anderson, Alex. *Rotary Cutting with Alex Anderson: Tips, Techniques, Projects.* Lafayette, CA: C&T Publishing, 1999.

Cory, Pepper. *Mastering Quilt Marking: Marking Tools and Techniques, Choosing Stencils, Matching Borders & Corners.* Lafayette, CA: C&T Publishing, 1999.

McClun, Diana and Nownes, Laura. *Quilts! Quilts!! Quilts!!! The Complete Guide to Quiltmaking.* Gualala, CA: Quilt Digest Press, 1988.

An Amish Adventure, 2nd Edition,
Roberta Horton

Appliqué 12 Easy Ways! Elly Sienkiewicz

The Art of Silk Ribbon Embroidery,
Judith Baker Montano

The Artful Ribbon, Candace Kling

At Home with Patrick Lose, Colorful Quilted Projects, Patrick Lose

Baltimore Album Legacy, Catalog of C&T Publishing's 1998 Baltimore Album Quilt Show and Contest, Elly Sienkiewicz

Baltimore Beauties and Beyond (Volume I),
Elly Sienkiewicz

Colors Changing Hue, Yvonne Porcella

Crazy Quilt Handbook, Judith Montano

Curves in Motion, Quilt Designs & Techniques, Judy B. Dales

Deidre Scherer, Work in Fabric and Thread,
Deidre Scherer

Dimensional Appliqué, Baskets, Blooms & Baltimore Borders, Elly Sienkiewicz

Easy Pieces, Creative Color Play with Two Simple Quilt Blocks, Margaret Miller

Elegant Stitches, An Illustrated Stitch Guide & Source Book of Inspiration,
Judith Baker Montano

Enduring Grace, Quilts from the Shelburne Museum Collection, Celia Y. Oliver

Everything Flowers, Quilts from the Garden,
Jean and Valori Wells

The Fabric Makes the Quilt, Roberta Horton

Free Stuff for Quilters on the Internet,
Judy Heim and Gloria Hansen

From Fiber to Fabric, The Essential Guide to Quiltmaking Textiles, Harriet Hargrave

Hand Quilting with Alex Anderson, Six Projects for Hand Quilters, Alex Anderson

Heirloom Machine Quilting, Third Edition,
Harriet Hargrave

Jacobean Rhapsodies, Composing with 28 Appliqué Designs, Patricia Campbell and Mimi Ayers

Judith B. Montano, Art & Inspirations,
Judith B. Montano

Make Any Block Any Size, Easy Drawing Method • Unlimited Pattern Possibilities • Sensational Quilt Designs, Joen Wolfrom

Mariner's Compass Quilts, New Directions,
Judy Mathieson

Mastering Machine Appliqué,
Harriet Hargrave

The New Sampler Quilt, Diana Leone

Papercuts and Plenty, Vol. III of Baltimore Beauties and Beyond, Elly Sienkiewicz

The Photo Transfer Handbook, Snap It, Print It, Stitch It! Jean Ray Laury

Piecing, Expanding the Basics,
Ruth B. McDowell

Plaids & Stripes, The Use of Directional Fabrics in Quilts, Roberta Horton

Quilts from the Civil War, Nine Projects, Historical Notes, Diary Entries,
Barbara Brackman

Quilts, Quilts, and More Quilts!
Diana McClun and Laura Nownes

Rotary Cutting with Alex Anderson, Tips • Techniques • Projects, Alex Anderson

Say It with Quilts, Diana McClun and Laura Nownes

Scrap Quilts, The Art of Making Do,
Roberta Horton

Simply Stars, Quilts that Sparkle,
Alex Anderson

Start Quilting with Alex Anderson, Six Projects for First-Time Quilters,
Alex Anderson

Through the Garden Gate, Quilters and Their Gardens, Jean and Valori Wells

Tradition with a Twist, Variations on Your Favorite Quilts, Blanche Young and Dalene Young Stone

Trapunto by Machine, Hari Walner

Wildflowers, Designs for Appliqué and Quilting, Carol Armstrong

Yvonne Porcella, Art & Inspirations

For more information write for a free catalog from:

C&T Publishing, Inc.

P.O. Box 1456
Lafayette, CA 94549
(800) 284-1114
http://www.ctpub.com
email: ctinfo@ctpub.com

The Cotton Patch Mail Order

3405 Hall Lane, Dept. CTB
Layayette, CA 94549
e-mail: cottonpa@aol.com
(800) 835-4418
(925) 283-7883
A Complete Quilting Supply Store

ABOUT THE AUTHOR

Jennifer Gilbert is the curator of the New England Quilt Museum in Lowell, MA. Jennifer grew up in Washington, D.C., where as a child she visited many museums here and abroad.

Her appreciation of art and interest in its producers led her to a traditional course in art history. Studying the evolution of the quilt has provided a fascinating look into the artistic lives of American quiltmakers both past and present.

RJR Fashion Fabrics has designed *The Lowell Collection,* a forty-one piece line of reproduction fabrics adapted from quilts housed in the New England Quilt Museum. Some of the motifs were recreated from prints contained in *Boston Pavement, Tumbling Blocks, Mini-Basket,* and *Variable Star.* Check with your local quilt shop or fabric store about he availabilty of the *The Lowell Collection* in your area.

INDEX